# ISRAEL AFTER THE SIX-D...

LEBANON

Metulla

SYRIA

Acre
Safed
Kuneitra
GOLAN
HEIGHTS

Haifa
Sea of
Galilee

Nazareth

N

Jenin
Nablus

River Jordan

MEDITERRANEAN

SEA

Tel Aviv-Jaffa
West
Bank

cLydda

Ashdod
Jericho

I S R A E L

Jerusalem

Gaza
Hebron

Dead
Sea

Khan Yunis
Rafah
Dimona

El Arish
Sdom

Romani
Nitsana

Port Said
Port Fuad

Kantara

SUEZ CANAL
Quseima

Ismailia

Bir Gifgafa
Jebel
Libni

Nile

J O R D A N

Suez
El Kuntilla

Port
Tewfik
Mitla Pass
Nakhl

EGYPT
Themed

Eilat
Akaba

SINAI

PENINSULA

GULF OF AKABA

Nuweiba

SAUDI

ARABIA

Gulf of Suez

0  10 20 30  40 50
Miles.

Mount
Sinai
Dahab

El Tur

SANAFIR

Straits of Tiran

Sharm
el Sheikh

e heavy outline shows the frontiers
Israel before June 5, 1967.
e shaded areas show the territory
cupied by Israel as a result of the
-Day War.

# MOSHE DAYAN

General Moshe Dayan

AFTER A PORTRAIT BY TOPOLSKI

# MOSHE DAYAN

## A BIOGRAPHY

## BY

## NAPHTALI LAU-LAVIE

Hartmore House Inc. Hartford

## ACKNOWLEDGEMENTS

Grateful acknowledgement is made for the use of the following illustrations:

Frontispiece: by kind permission of the artist, Feliks Topolski.

Dayan, aged three (facing p. 16) and Dayan's family (facing p. 161) by kind permission of Routledge and Kegan Paul Ltd.

Dayan in Vietnam (facing p. 160) by kind permission of *The Sunday Telegraph*.

Generals Dayan, Rabin and Hod at Victory parade (facing p. 177) by kind permission of Camera Press Ltd.

Dayan addressing Arab leaders in Gaza (facing p. 176) by kind permission of United Press International (U.K.) Ltd.

Book design by Jesse Zierler
SBN: 85303 004 9

First published in Great Britain in 1968 by Vallentine, Mitchell & Co. Ltd., 18 Cursitor Street, London E.C.4
Second impression 1969

Printed in Great Britain by Tonbridge Printers Ltd., Tonbridge, Kent

# CONTENTS

# ILLUSTRATIONS

# INTRODUCTION

MOSHE DAYAN once compared himself to the sons of Zeruiah, whom King David reproached for their hardness. The best known of Zeruiah's sons was Joab, the king's great military commander and the hammer of the Philistines. Dayan was replying at the time to David Ben-Gurion, who had told him of complaints about his, Dayan's, alleged ruthlessness and obstinacy.

The insinuation was not lost on the 'Old Man', who had himself singled out Dayan to be a leader. Ben-Gurion knew that, when it was a matter of national security, Dayan could indeed be ruthless, even towards those closest to him. When Dayan resigned as Chief of Staff of Israel's Armed Forces in January 1958, Ben-Gurion, then Prime Minister, summed up his qualities in a few words:

'You have two diametrically opposed facets to your character – courage bordering upon the lunatic, offset and balanced by a profound tactical and strategic intelligence.'

Ben-Gurion apart, no public figure in modern Israel has aroused more passionate admiration, or more bitter hostility, than Moshe Dayan. Many of Israel's senior politicians – leaders of the Mapai group to which Dayan formerly belonged – regard him as a tempestuous man, indifferent towards the beliefs and institutions they have cherished since the early days of pioneering socialist Zionism. Veteran ideologists from Eastern Europe dis-

9

like the aggressive iconoclasm of this fifty-three-year-old Sabra (Israel-born Jew) and farmer's son and fear his political ambitions.

However Dayan's is exactly the sort of personality that appeals to his fellow Sabras. They see in him a determined fighter with a similar background to their own, unlike many of the older Zionist leaders; a man who speaks their own language.

Their confidence in him was amply demonstrated in the days preceding the Six-Day War. When in May 1967, President Nasser faced Israel with the gravest crisis since her establishment nineteen years before – with seven Egyptian divisions standing at war strength on her southern frontier and Arab spokesmen threatening her with annihilation – the country was governed by a Cabinet many of whose members were advanced in years, and who the public felt were not able to give the determined and decisive leadership that the rapidly deteriorating situation required. Israelis believed that Nasser had carefully studied the weaknesses of their leaders in timing his challenge, and their anxieties were not allayed by prolonged haggling between the political parties over the formation of a National Government.

In that moment of near-despair, public demand for the appointment of Moshe Dayan as Defence Minister developed spontaneously into a national movement. The masses wanted Dayan because of his personal charisma, his decisiveness, and also because of their natural feeling that the man who had defeated the Egyptians in Sinai in 1956 could do it again. When, three days after Dayan's appointment, war began, there was a universal feeling that the country now had a competent and able leader.

In the event, this feeling was fully justified, as Dayan's advocacy was the deciding factor in triggering the action against Egypt, and he himself also contributed much to the achievement of the Israeli forces.

But, despite his toughness of mind and manner, Moshe Dayan is a deeply sensitive and warm-hearted man. His attitude towards prisoners of war and Arab civilians in the territories occupied after the fighting bears out the fact that he also has a strong sense of justice. While energetically combating terrorist activities, he has maintained a liberal policy towards the people of the occupied areas, leaving them as far as possible to run their own affairs and allowing commercial and social relations with the Kingdom of Jordan.

Although he is not religious, Dayan was among the first at the Wailing Wall after the capture of the Old City of Jerusalem. There he wrote a prayer on a slip of paper and thrust it between the ancient stones, according to the custom followed by religious Jews for centuries. His prayer was: 'Let there be everlasting peace upon Israel.'

# 1
## Family of Aristocrats

IF THE NEW and egalitarian society of Israel can be said
to have an aristocracy, then it consists of those people
who, like Moshe Dayan's parents, emigrated to Palestine
from Tsarist Russia in the years between the Russo-
Japanese War in 1905 and the outbreak of the First
World War in 1914. They formed what is known in
Zionist annals as the Second Aliyah. (Aliyah is a Hebrew
word meaning ascent or immigration to Israel.) In all,
35,000 Jews from Russia and the Ukraine took part in it,
most of them youngsters. They included rabbinical
students who had left the yeshiva (Talmudic seminary)
and university students sick of the antisemitism they
found among their contemporaries. Of this comparatively
small body of immigrants not all stayed in Palestine,
but those who did looked upon themselves as being, like
the American Pilgrim Fathers, a cut above all who
followed them. Today, fifty or sixty years later, their
attitude remains the same.

It was the immigrants of the Second Aliyah who gave
to the Jewish community in Palestine the socialist character which it was, in large measure, to retain through the
years of British rule and of independent statehood. They
founded the Histadrut, the trade union organisation,
which later grew into the most powerful economic force
in the country. Influenced by both Marxist and Tol-

stoyan ideas, they established the first of the communal agricultural settlements known as kibbutzim.

Shmuel Dayan was born in 1891 the son of the rabbi of a small town near Kiev, the Ukrainian capital. He was given a religious education but, when only 15, he joined the Zionist socialist movement which had begun to organise itself in Russian and Ukrainian towns. At the age of 17 he left his father's home and went to Palestine, which was then under Turkish rule.

Like many of the pioneer immigrants of those days (among them David Ben-Gurion and later Levi Eshkol), the intelligent young man from the Ukraine became a farm labourer. He worked for farmers at Petach Tikva, a settlement founded towards the end of the last century by Hungarian-born Jews from Jerusalem, and at other Jewish settlements, where physically strong young people like himself were sorely needed. But Shmuel Dayan wanted to work his own land and not that of others. He decided to move northwards. In the valley of Jezreel (Esdraelon), in those days a desolate area, he came across the settlement of Yavne'el, where he found employment. From there he moved further north, to the settlement of Kinneret, near the Sea of Galilee. There he made friends with a group of more recent arrivals from Russia and the Ukraine and, together with them, he founded, not far away, the communal settlement of Degania. It was the very first kibbutz.

The kibbutzim were to become a prominent, and unique, feature of Jewish society in Palestine. Their basic principle is complete collectivisation of property within the settlement. In the early days this applied not only to land, equipment and buildings but even to such personal belongings as socks and shirts. Even today, in the majority of kibbutzim in Israel, meals are eaten communally in a dining hall and children sleep together in their own houses. Inside a kibbutz money never changes hands. All decisions are taken by a majority vote of members. Today these may number, in the case of any particular kibbutz, many hundreds, but at first it was thought important to maintain the face-to-face character of the community by imposing a low ceiling on membership. For this reason, Degania, which, when Shmuel Dayan helped to found it, consisted of a mere handful of members, was later to divide itself, after numbers had grown, into two adjacent but separate settlements, Degania Aleph and Degania Bet.

Shmuel Dayan, then still under twenty, was one of the pillars of the new settlement, which, to begin with, was so poor that the same old building had to house both the farmers and their cattle. At the same time, he began to try his hand at journalism, writing articles and reports which were published in several newspapers and periodicals. With other members of the settlement he helped to found a movement called Hapoel Hatzair (literally The Young Worker). This later merged with the Poalei Zion (Workers of Zion) movement, of which David Ben-Gurion was one of the founders. It was this merger which produced Mapai (the name was formed from the initials of the words *Mifleget Poalei Eretz Israel*, meaning the Palestine Workers' Party) which was to become the largest political party in Israel. Both Ben-Gurion and Shmuel Dayan were to quit the party they had established, but not until some fifty years later.

Devora Zatolovsky was also a native of the Ukraine.

Her father was a Zionist intellectual and a writer in both Russian and Hebrew. Devora received a Hebrew education and herself became a teacher. She lived with her parents in the small town of Poltava until she emigrated in 1913 to Palestine, where she and Shmuel Dayan met. The following year they married and settled down in Degania, where they were to stay for the next seven years. Their first child was born in 1915, and they named him Moshe, after a member of the kibbutz who had been murdered shortly before by Arab marauders.

During the First World War, with the British Forces under General Allenby harrassing the Turks in Palestine, Degania became a transit camp for thousands of Jews whom the Turkish authorities deported to the north of the country. They were suspected of pro-British leanings. The kibbutz became a place of refuge where the deportees obtained aid and sustenance before moving on.

Almost the only memory Moshe retains of his early childhood in Degania is of a punishment given him by his father for disobedience. When writers for youth magazines ask him what sort of a child he was, Moshe Dayan will invariably grin cheekily and say he was always good, helped his parents and took care of his younger sister, Aviva. When the mood takes him, however, he will also tell how one night, when he was five years old, his father locked him in the chicken coop for not doing what he was told. Little Moshe trembled with fright at the strange sounds inside the coop and all around it. There were many jackals prowling about in the neighbourhood. But the child did not capitulate. He sat there shivering in the dark until a few hours later his father released him, not a whit less obstinate than when

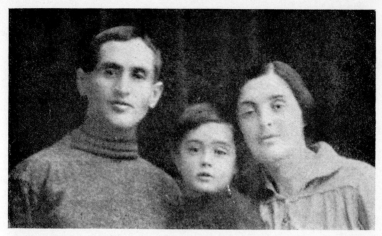

Moshe Dayan, aged three, with his parents in Degania in 1918

The young Dayan (standing, left) with schoolfriends, Nahalal 1931

Aged fifteen, on patrol at Nahalal in 1930

Sergeant Dayan of the Palestine
Supernumerary Police

he had gone in. Moshe claims that this was one of the events which moulded his personality.

After the end of the First World War, Shmuel Dayan decided the time had come for him to start his own farm and reap the rewards of his own labour. But the country, now under British Mandatory rule, was going through hard times, and it was impossible for him to raise the necessary money. He therefore conceived the idea of founding a co-operative village where members would work their farms together and market their produce collectively but where each would eat his own meals in his own home, bring up his children as he wished and in general live the life of his choice. He found sufficient friends ready to follow his lead.

At the western approaches to the bleak Valley of Jezreel, this group of friends founded Nahalal in 1921. Nahalal was the first moshav, or smallholders' co-operative village. Today there are some hundreds of moshavim throughout Israel, forming one of the most important elements in the country's economy.

The Dayans and their fellow settlers worked hard from dawn to dusk, but, while determined to root themselves in the soil of their country, they endeavoured to maintain their high cultural standards. Some of them, including both Shmuel and Devora Dayan, took up writing, both poetry and prose. For the children, a village school was set up, where Moshe Dayan received his basic education. As the children grew older, the problem arose of how to enable them to continue their studies, as there was no secondary school in Nahalal or its immediate vicinity.

A solution to the problem came through the decision

of the WIZO, the Women's International Zionist Organisation, to establish an Agricultural School for Girls from Palestine and Overseas who wished to settle on the land and help their future husbands to run their farms. This was the era when Zionist aspirations centred on building up the agricultural settlements. The farmers of Nahalal agreed that the girls' boarding school should be built in their village, and in 1926 the school was opened by its founder and first headmistress, Mrs Hannah Maisel-Shochet. In addition to a general education in the humanities, instruction was given in such subjects as botany, zoology, chemistry and physics. The people of Nahalal were favourably impressed and asked permission for their sons to attend the school, as well as their daughters. The first boy to be accepted into the girls' school was Moshe Dayan.

Mrs Maisel-Shochet, who now lives in retirement in Tel Aviv, well remembers the school's early days before Moshe joined. The boys of Nahalal were renowned for their mischievousness and were not easily disciplined. Moshe was the ringleader, and the boys would often play pranks on the girls and even make raids on the school. On one occasion the headmistress threw them out of the school grounds, and in retaliation they broke the windows of one of the classrooms. Mrs Maisel-Shochet complained to the village council, but the farmers were at a loss to know how to curb their young sons' exuberance. However, Moshe Dayan turned up at the headmistress's office and told her the boys would pay for the damage and would no longer disturb the peace of the school. The headmistress looked the youngster straight in the eye and saw that he not only meant what he said but was obviously a leader who could control his friends and influence them towards doing the right thing. Later the school accepted him, and he became one of its best pupils.

Just occasionally he would play practical jokes, like the time when he caught a snake in a field and released it in a classroom full of girls who ran, screaming, for their lives. But such episodes were rare, and in general he was shy and reserved in the company of the opposite sex.

Outside school Moshe kept his leadership of the village boys. His friends, who were all older than he, admired him for his strong physique, for his loyalty towards them, and for his initiative in planning and carrying out the pranks they played on the older farmers in Nahalal and the nearby villages. Whenever they decided to hold a picnic around a campfire at night, Moshe would organise a foray into the vineyard of a neighbouring village and emerge with boxes of grapes to be eaten before the picnic was over.

Moshe was still under 13 when he got his first taste of the battle for national survival, which he was to pursue for the next forty years. The boy, on his white mare, accompanied by several friends on horseback, had ridden out of Nahalal for a canter across the fields. When they were some distance from home, the youngsters spotted a herd of Arab cattle grazing in fields belonging to the moshav. Guarding the herd were four young Arabs. Moshe did not hesitate for a moment. Spurring his horse, he galloped full tilt into the midst of the herd, cracking his whip to right and left and scattering the cattle in all directions. The young Arabs were taken by surprise, but fury blazed in their eyes. Moshe made a second dash amongst the animals to make quite sure they were off his village's land, and then the Arabs leaped on him. They dragged Moshe off his mare and on to the ground. He struggled furiously, but they were too many for him, and he was badly beaten.

His companions, meanwhile, galloped off to call for help from the village. By the time they returned, Moshe was covered in blood. 'Don't get excited about it,' he advised, 'learn a lesson from it. Next time we bring sticks instead of whips.' The Arabs and their herd had vanished and Moshe told his friends confidently: 'They won't dare trespass on our land again.'

His courage and decisiveness earned him a reputation in the area, even though his action was looked upon by the village elders as irresponsible.

Although Moshe's forceful character and single-mindedness manifested themselves when he was still a boy, one handicap from which he suffered was his manner of speech. His words sounded confused and laborious and his sentences disorganised, making it difficult to grasp exactly what it was he was driving at. He appeared to compose his thoughts as he spoke. Traces of this habit remained with him even in later life, when great importance was attached to anything he said or hinted. But the exact opposite was true of his writing, which was lucid, smooth, stylish and simple. His talent for writing, which he showed even as a youngster at school, was doubtlessly inherited from his parents, and particularly from his mother. From early childhood he adored his mother. For his father he had great respect, and he claims to have inherited from Shmuel Dayan much of his own strength of character. Although at times his father punished him for disobedience, he was also very affectionate and spoiled him considerably.

As far as his reading was concerned, the young Moshe enjoyed the great Russian authors, Tolstoy, Dostoevsky, Gorky and Pushkin. But he was not academically inclined and did not go to university after graduating from the Agricultural School in Nahalal. Only after many years was he to find the time to renew his studies.

It was at the Agricultural School that Moshe met Ruth Schwarz, daughter of Dr Zvi Schwarz, a well-to-do Jerusalem lawyer, originally from Bessarabia. Ruth had become infected with the pioneering urge of the era which brought many youngsters out of the cities and into the villages. She wanted to learn agriculture and become a farmer's wife, which was why she went to Nahalal after studying at the Hebrew High School in the middle-class Jerusalem district of Rehavia. Moshe Dayan swept her off her feet but upset her parents considerably. They would have liked her to marry a university graduate with an assured future, not a young farmer from Nahalal. His rough-and-ready ways might not endear him to the upper crust of Jerusalem society. But the young couple adamantly insisted on marrying, and the only concession they were willing to make to Ruth's parents was to spend a short time in England, where Moshe could learn English and perhaps acquire a little Western polish. The wedding took place in July, 1935. After a seven-month honeymoon in London, the young couple built a hut for themselves at Nahalal.

The farm which Shmuel Dayan had established assured his son and daughter-in-law of a livelihood. The farm was now, in fact, managed by Moshe, as both his parents spent much time away from Nahalal. They were active in Zionist affairs, Shmuel being one of the leaders of the Moshav Movement, the umbrella organisation set up by the smallholders' co-operatives. For a time Devora helped her husband to run the Movement's journal. Their two other children, Aviva and Zohar (Moshe's brother, born in 1926), were not yet grown up, so full responsibility for the farm fell upon Moshe. When there was little to do there, he and a group of friends would travel to Tel Aviv in search of work. During the building boom of the thirties, these young men formed themselves into a co-operative and built houses in the city. They would return to Nahalal for the harvest and, when the crops had been gathered in, set about erecting brick houses for the farmers, who up till then had lived in wooden huts.

# 2

## In League against the Common Foe

WHILE STILL A youth, Moshe Dayan became active in
the Haganah, the clandestine defence organisation of
the Jewish community in Palestine. The Haganah (the
word means defence) was founded in 1920 and super-
seded other Jewish organisations which had grown up to
protect the settlers against Arab bandits. But with the
expulsion of the Turks and the beginning of large-scale
Jewish immigration under the British Mandatory Government, Arab violence assumed a more serious character,
and the need for self-protection grew correspondingly
urgent. Bloody riots occurred in 1929, when Arab bands
attacked Jewish settlements and slaughtered the Jews of
Hebron. However, there followed seven years of com-
parative calm. It was a period of mass immigration of
Jews from Poland, seeking a refuge in Palestine from the
political and economic disabilities imposed upon them
by the Polish Government. The period also witnessed
the arrival of the first waves of immigrants from Germany, where the Nazis came to power in 1933. During
these years many kibbutzim were established by young
pioneers who had organised themselves into groups
before leaving Poland, Germany, Austria and elsewhere,
and who were allocated land bought by the Jewish
National Fund. One of these kibbutzim was Kfar
Hahoresh, founded in 1933, in the hills between Nazareth

23

and Nahalal. The young pioneers invited Moshe to instruct and advise them in organising a system of defence for their new home.

Between 1933 and 1936 about 165,000 European Jews settled in Palestine. This new influx of immigrants brought home to Arab nationalist leaders the reality of what was happening in the country, where the Jews were threatening to become a majority. In 1936 fresh Arab riots broke out, and in May the Arab leaders declared a general strike in an attempt to induce the British authorities to curb Jewish immigration. Hitherto the British had endeavoured, with great caution, to administer Palestine in the spirit of the 1917 Balfour Declaration which promised to establish a national home for the Jews in that country. But in November 1936, six months after the beginning of the Arab general strike, a Royal Commission was set up under Lord Peel to inquire into the tense situation which had arisen as a result of Arab opposition to Jewish immigration and the sale of land to Jews. The Peel Commission recommended a temporary solution which, in effect, would restrict Jewish immigration and put a stop to the settlement of Jews on the land. A longer-range proposal called for the partitioning of the country into a Jewish State and an Arab State, both of which would be linked to Britain by military and economic agreements.

Meanwhile, conditions continued to deteriorate. They reached flashpoint in the summer of 1937 with the publication of the Peel Report. The Arabs' reaction to the report was to convert their strike into armed insurgency, directed at Jews and British alike. This was the Arab rebellion, which was to continue unabated until

the outbreak of the Second World War in 1939.
Until the Arab rebellion the Jewish leaders had
followed a policy of restraint towards Arab belligerency.
The tactics adopted were those of passive defence. Only
on rare occasions had the Jews overstepped the official
line and taken punitive measures against Arab terrorists. With the upsurge of violence in 1936, however,
some Jewish leaders, among them David Ben-Gurion,
demanded a more aggressive policy and the introduction
of punitive counter-attacks. Others, including Shmuel
Dayan and Pinhas Lavon, later to become Minister of
Defence in independent Israel, advocated a continuance
of the policy of restraint.

The 'doves' believed that co-operation with the
British was still possible, despite the keen disappointment felt at the negative turn taken by British policy
regarding Jewish aspirations in Palestine. They emphasised the sympathetic attitude shown by the Mandatory
Government over the problem of safeguarding the
Jewish population against Arab violence, in particular
by the formation of the Supernumerary Police. This
quasi-military Jewish force was set up under the command of the British Palestine Police to help Jewish settlements against attack. The 'hawks', led by Ben-Gurion,
while rejecting further restraint, were ready to use this
opportunity, provided by the British, to strengthen the
Haganah. Several thousand Haganah volunteers joined
the Supernumerary Police, which served as a legal
framework for the Jewish defence force. While operating
under British auspices, these volunteers in fact took their
orders from the Haganah. In 1937, units of the Supernumerary Police were organised into mobile squads.

These, instead of relying on the old tactics of holding static defence positions and waiting to be attacked, developed a technique of ambushing Arab marauders. This proved much more effective.

It was while Moshe Dayan was still on his honeymoon visit to England that the 1936 troubles began. The Haganah recalled him to Palestine, and his plans for staying in England to study agriculture had to be scrapped. Once back home, he was ordered to enlist in the Supernumerary Police. By 1938 he had risen to be an instructor, training sergeants for the auxiliary force. In the same year the Haganah organised its own Field Platoons, under the command of the legendary Yitzhak Sadeh, who was to become one of the greatest Israeli commanders in the 1948 War of Independence. The Field Platoons, in which men served for six months at a time, specialised in carrying out surprise attacks against the Arab terrorist bands. Two of the platoon leaders selected by Sadeh to be his deputies were Moshe Dayan and another young Sabra, Moshe's junior by three years, Yigal Allon. These two men who now met, for the first time, as comrades-in-arms were to become in the years ahead political opponents and rivals for national leadership.

Allon was born at Kfar Tabor, in Galilee. His grand-parents, from Russia, were among the founders of Rosh Pinna, the first Jewish settlement in Upper Galilee, and he himself helped to found Kibbutz Ginossar in 1937. He was to remain a kibbutznik throughout his career, rising to become a leader of the Ahdut Avoda (Unity of Labour) party which drew its chief strength from the kibbutzim. This party, which began as a Left-wing faction of Mapai, was later to split away from it and still later to return to alliance with it. Besides his political struggles, Allon was also to play a notable part in Israel's War of Independence. But in 1938 all that lay far in the future.

It was in March of that year that the two young Haganah commanders were given the first opportunity to show their mettle. In defiance of Britain's new policy of preventing further Jewish settlement on the land, and regardless of the bellicose threats of the local Arabs, it had been decided to establish a kibbutz in the hills of Western Galilee, on the Lebanese border. The only way of creating a Jewish settlement in those days was by a *fait accompli*. To cope with this situation the so-called 'Tower and Fence' system had been evolved. Acting at lightning speed, a group of settlers would take possession of their land overnight and by dawn would have erected a watch-tower, a building and a few tents, with a fence surrounding them all. Such a procedure was essential to ensure the settlement's survival.

The rocky terrain where the new settlement was to be established was extremely difficult to defend. In fact there were serious doubts as to whether it would be possible to finish everything by morning. Nevertheless, it was considered vital to go ahead with the project. The background to this decision was the 1937 British restriction on Jewish settlement in Palestine. David Ben-Gurion, who was then in charge of security and defence matters in the Jewish Agency and thus responsible for Haganah activities, had said that Jewish land holdings in Galilee must be safeguarded by the establishment of four or five new settlements. The Haganah, therefore, mobilised its best fighters for the operation.

On a spring night in March 1938, a convoy of pack-horses, laden with the equipment needed to establish the settlement, wound its way up the narrow mountain paths. Accompanying the men and women who were to make their home on the frontier were two Haganah platoons, commanded by Dayan and Allon. Ruth Dayan also was present and became, with her husband, one of the first settlers.

Violent opposition by Arab bands who operated in the area and from over the borders, was expected. The site of the new settlement was reached. The fortifications were nowhere near completion when, at midnight, the Arabs struck. Their attack was concentrated and powerful, but every attempt to storm the settlement was successfully repulsed by the young defenders, firing from their half-finished fortified positions. The Arabs finally withdrew and returned to their villages to lick their wounds; they had inflicted only minor casualties upon the settlers. Four days later a new, and vastly larger, wave of attackers appeared, led this time by one of the Arab terrorist chiefs. The Haganah commanders decided to carry the battle to the enemy by staging an all-out counter-attack, using 'hammer and anvil' tactics. The role of the 'anvil' was to ambush the enemy force and keep it in an area where the 'hammer' could swoop down and crush it. Dayan's platoon, acting as the 'hammer', took the Arab marauders completely by surprise. The Arabs were routed, and Hanita, the settlement estab-lished beside the Lebanese hills, still stands there today and looks down southwards across the State of Israel.

Despite this and other successes, the British Army and

the police were incapable of preventing Arab attacks from spreading throughout the country. From month to month they grew in ferocity. Haganah headquarters began enlisting men for training and established a cadre of officers capable of handling new and more sophisticated weapons. The first training course in the use of these weapons, as well as in that of mines and communications equipment, was of a high standard but restricted to a very small group of 'students'. Among them were Yigal Allon and Moshe Dayan.

That spring of 1938 saw the emergence of a new and important factor in the military situation. Special Night Squads were formed by an extraordinary British Army intelligence officer, Captain Orde Charles Wingate. Wingate had been sent to Palestine in 1936 and had quickly managed to gain the respect and confidence of the Jews. They found in him a true and brave ally, ready to fight even his superiors in his efforts to suppress Arab terrorism. He earned from the Jews the sobriquet of Hayedid (The Friend), and among the initiated of the Haganah he was always referred to by that name.

Orde Wingate was a deeply religious man, well versed in the Bible; his Bible was always with him as he walked the highways and byways of the country, trying to identify the sites mentioned and described therein. To Wingate the task assigned to him of combating Arab insurgency was a mystical mission. He was enthralled with the account, in Chapter VII of the Book of Judges, of Gideon's heroism and military victories. Wingate set up his headquarters at Ein Harod, where the camp of Gideon had been in Biblical times. His Night Squads were composed of a few British regulars and a much

larger number of Haganah men, including members of
the Supernumerary Police. Wingate's art of warfare
called for swift mobility and sharp thrusts into the
marauders' bases before they could set out on their
expeditions of terror and sabotage. After an intensive
six-week course of training, Wingate launched his men
on the night-fighting operations for which they shortly
became renowned.

Their first assignment was to guard the oil pipeline
from Iraq to Haifa. This pipeline was a constant target
for Arab attackers who blew it up and set fire to the oil.
Wingate did not remain in close proximity to the pipeline he had to guard, for that was where the Arabs lay in
ambush for the unwary. He led his men straight into the
villages where the saboteurs were known to concentrate.
These operations built up the strength of Wingate's
Jewish troops who had to emulate his powers of en-
durance, his speed and his tenacity in keeping to his
objective although lying in ambush for lengthy periods.
They also became accustomed to night fighting. One of
those who fought under Wingate was Moshe Dayan, who
commanded a company of Supernumerary Police, and a
great friendship sprang up between the two men. Dayan
was greatly impressed by the Englishman and learnt
much from him in military skill, audacity and resourcefulness.

Their friendship, which developed during the nocturnal ambushes and forays in which they fought together,
led Dayan to accompany Wingate on almost every
mission. He became his aide-de-camp, and between
them they fought one of the biggest and fiercest battles
against the Arabs. Near a village in the Hills of Ephraim,

they put to rout a large terrorist band operating under the command of Abu Dura, one of the most daring of the Arab rebels.

Dayan and Wingate had a warm regard for each other. In conversation the Englishman would often refer to his friend, Dayan, and on more than one occasion said of him that he was a fine soldier who would one day bring great victories to the people of Israel.

Wingate, however, did not last long in Palestine. The British authorities disapproved of his championship of the Zionist cause and his intimate friendship with a Jewish combatant. In 1939 Wingate was recalled to England. Later he fought in Ethiopia and in Burma and finally met his death when the 'plane in which he was flying crashed in the Burmese jungle. Dayan was left to continue the battle with other members of the Haganah. But now their operations were clandestine, for the British had withdrawn their patronage.

The existence of an organised military force operating under the direction of the Jewish Agency worried the British. They followed the movements of Haganah units, even those operating within the framework of the Supernumerary Police. As a result of their vigilance they discovered the location of an officers' course the Haganah was giving. The trainees moved from place to place in an effort to shake off any snoopers, but finally the British managed to take them by surprise. It was September 1939, and ninety of the most promising and capable of the Haganah's young men were taking part in the course. One group escaped the British ambush, but a second group was surrounded and taken into custody. At their trial forty-three participants in the course were

31

sentenced to varying terms in prison. Among the officer-instructors who were caught and tried was Moshe Dayan. He was sentenced to five years' imprisonment.

The Jewish community was shocked at the news of the sentences given to the young Haganah commanders. This hostile act raised grave doubts about the possibility of continued co-operation with the British. The feeling of concern was greatly enhanced by the fact that at that time world Jewry stood shoulder to shoulder with the free countries of the world, including Britain, in their fight against Hitler. Ben-Gurion called upon the General Officer Commanding the British Forces in Palestine, and asked that his men be released. Instead of discussing their release, however, the British General demanded the immediate disbandment of the Haganah. Completely forgotten was the fact that only a few weeks previously the Haganah had co-operated with the British forces in a joint operational endeavour to bring the Arab rebellion to an end.

But there were people of importance in England who did not approve of this aggressive policy towards the Haganah. Field-Marshal Lord Ironside, Chief of the Imperial General Staff, expressed sympathy for Ben-Gurion's request when the two men met in London and the Jewish leader asked for the British Army chief's intervention on behalf of the imprisoned Haganah men. When Ironside heard that one of the detainees was a young fellow named Moshe Dayan, who had been a pupil and colleague of Orde Wingate, the Field-Marshal commented with an ironic smile: 'Fancy, they have condemned one of Wingate's lads to imprisonment. He ought to have been given the D.S.O.' Ironside then

)ayan (left) with Yitzhak Sadeh and Yigal Allon in the Haganah at Hanita 1938

t. Colonel Dayan with Colonel el Tel, Military Governor of Jordanian Jerusalem 1948

Receiving President and Mrs Weizmann on their first official visit to Jerusalem 1949 (on left, Dov Yosef, Military Governor of the City)

Lt. Colonel Dayan with U.N. observer at the time of the Jordanian withdrawal from Wadi Ara, near Tulkarem, May 1949

quietly whispered in Ben-Gurion's ear: 'What a damn stupid sentence to have given!'

As was to have been expected, the imprisonment of the forty-three members of the Haganah brought about a transformation in the relations between the heads of the Jewish community in Palestine and the British authorities. Jewish bitterness against the Mandatory Government had already mounted in May 1939, with the publication of the White Paper on Palestine which restricted the possibilities of Jewish development in the country and placed in jeopardy the hopes of establishing the Jewish National Home. The prison sentences widened the breach, and as a result the possibility of armed resistance to the British forces in Palestine began to take shape in the minds of the Haganah.

Moshe Dayan and his forty-two companions, including Moshe Carmel (today Minister of Transport in the Israeli Government) were imprisoned in the ancient fortress of Acre which had so successfully withstood a sixty-one day siege by Napoleon I in 1799. They shared with criminals and Arab terrorist leaders the dank, bleak gaol the outer walls of which are pounded by the Mediterranean. There the forty-three organised themselves in a way which was later to serve as an example and inspiration to the young generation who took up the fight for Israel's independence. Dayan quite naturally became the chief and spokesman of the Jewish detainees without anyone having elected or appointed him to the post. He earned the reputation of being a cool-headed leader, respected because of the way he consulted his companions, his forceful attitude towards the hostile prison authorities and his decisiveness in dealing with the belliggerence of the Arab prisoners with whom the Jews shared quarters. But he gained the hearts of his companions mainly by his pungent and sardonic sense of humour and by his resourcefulness in saving himself and others from tight corners.

While Ruth Dayan and her baby daughter Yael, born at the beginning of 1939, waited in their wooden cottage in Nahalal, Moshe sat in prison in Acre perfecting his English. He also learnt various Arabic dialects and even adopted certain Arab habits and mannerisms. He spent much of his time writing poetry which, till today, he has kept hidden away. His favourite reading in prison was the works of Natan Alterman, a Hebrew poet and political writer, whose writings gave forceful expression to the emotional revulsion of the Jews in Palestine at the destruction of European Jewry, and to their feelings of bitter disappointment at the frustration of their aspirations towards an independent Jewish State.

Although the young men remained in prison, planning the struggle they knew they would face in the future, unceasing efforts were being made outside to obtain their release. A suitable opportunity presented itself early in 1941. At this time a threat to Britain's position in Palestine arose from the fact that Syria and the Lebanon were occupied by Vichy French forces, which were collaborating with Nazi Germany. British Headquarters were worried at the existence of hostile troop concentrations along Palestine's frontiers and realised the necessity for the speedy conquest of the two neighbouring countries before they could be used by a German army attacking southwards while Rommel's forces put pressure on British defences in the Western

Desert. The Jewish community in Palestine became a major factor in British military planning because of its natural anxiety at the terrible threat posed by the existence of Nazi collaborators only a few miles to the north.

From overtures made by representatives of the Jewish Agency to British Regional Headquarters, it was obvious that both the military and British intelligence were interested in having the assistance of the Jews in their operation against the Vichy forces. The British made it clear that what they wanted was a swift, clean operation with a minimum of bloodshed on either side. They had agreed to the request of General Charles de Gaulle, commander of the Free French forces, to bring about the surrender of Vichy forces in the Levant. To that end they had drawn up plans for the speedy conquest of both Syria and the Lebanon. With the help of Palestinian Jews, the British hoped to find the easiest means of access into enemy territory, in order to destroy French military installations in both countries. A further mission assigned to the Jewish advance commando force was the protection of roads and bridges to prevent the French from destroying them before withdrawing in face of invading British forces. The forty-three men detained in Acre were released early in 1941, some sixteen months after entering prison.

The first stage of the joint operation against the Vichy forces in the Levant had already been carried out at the end of 1940, when a twelve-member Jewish force penetrated Syria, disguised as Arabs, for the purpose of intelligence and espionage. The commander of that force was Tuvia Arazi, a Haganah man who later became Israel's Minister to Cyprus. When finally the Vichy authorities

35

caught him, Arazi was subjected to terrible torture for serving General de Gaulle. Eventually he succeeded in escaping and returned to Palestine.

British-Jewish co-operation continued with a seaborne mission to penetrate the Lebanese port of Tripoli and blow up the oil refineries there. On May 18, 1941, a small vessel, the *Sea Lion*, sailed from Haifa with twenty-three of the Haganah's best men on board. Their commander was Zvi Spector and they were accompanied by an observer from British military intelligence. The *Sea Lion* disappeared with all hands, and its fate has never been discovered.

By April 1941, British Headquarters had already completed its plans for the invasion of Syria and the Lebanon. Army liaison officers contacted David Hacohen, who was then the representative of the Jewish Agency's defence and security department, with a request to activate the promised assistance.

Two units of Jewish fighters were needed for the operation, and the commanders selected were, once again, Moshe Dayan and Yigal Allon, the former for his daring and courage and the latter for his prudence. These two officers divided the northern area of the country between them. Dayan was given the western sector from Haifa to the Lebanese border, while Allon had the eastern area from Tiberias to Metulla on the frontier with both Lebanon and Syria. Both commanders travelled among the kibbutzim and villages interviewing volunteers. After careful selection they each chose a complement of about thirty men.

The invasion operation was placed in the hands of General Sir Henry 'Jumbo' Maitland Wilson. As an invasion force he was given the 7th Australian Division plus an Indian infantry brigade, two brigades of Free French forces and several smaller units. The entire force consisted of fifteen battalions at full strength with a few tanks. Against them were thirty battalions of Vichy troops and ninety tanks.

Dayan concentrated his force at Hanita, on the Lebanese border (where he and his wife had lived for a time, three years before, and where he had first demonstrated his abilities as a combat officer). The British Army supplied neither arms nor any other equipment to the Haganah men, amongst whom was Yitzhak Rabin (who was to become Israel's Chief of Staff before, during and after the Six-Day War in June 1967). They used arms provided for them by the Haganah. Even identification discs were not given to them and, had they been caught by the Vichy troops, they would have been executed as spies. Inside the pockets of their khaki shirts, the men carried a slip of paper on which was written: 'The bearer is a Jewish resident of Palestine aiding British Forces in operations against Vichy French troops stationed in Syria and the Lebanon who are collaborators of Hitler Germany.' Whoever drafted this note obviously did not take into account the possibility that the Vichy French themselves might read it and be even more inclined to shoot the Jews as spies.

The two Haganah units did not have time for proper training. Dayan, however, knew which fighters were most suited for the operation. Racing around in his car through the Jewish settlements in the Valley of Jezreel and Western Galilee, he sought them out. One of them was Zalman Mart, who is today a lieutenant-colonel

37

in the Israeli Army with many military operations
behind him. He still remembers the Lebanese campaign
and what preceded it. Moshe Dayan turned up at his
house one morning and casually asked him if he would
like to see how the Australians fought the French.
Mart's curiosity was piqued and he jumped into Dayan's
car. When they reached Hanita he saw the preparations
being made and was given last-minute briefing.

Dayan's unit had the job of guiding the Allied forces
into Lebanese territory. At least that was what the Australian commanding officer thought. But neither Dayan
nor his men knew anything about the terrain they had
to pass through, so they engaged an Arab guide from
Haifa. One night before the operation the men were
given a topography briefing and early next morning they
set out on a reconnaissance patrol of the area.

The invasion was set for the night of June 8, 1941.
Dayan's men had been making nightly patrols across
the border for ten successive nights beforehand to check
whether the French were preparing to mine the Iskanderun Bridge and destroy it before retreating. They also
checked the easiest means of reaching their objective,
made estimates of the French strength there and left a
party near the bridge to prevent it being blown up at the
last minute before the Australian force arrived.

Dayan describes the days preceding this campaign
with considerable amusement. Not only were he and his
men hindered by British frontier guards who were un-
willing to accept their special passes and allow them to
cross into the Lebanon, they also found out that the
Arab guide employed to lead them to their objective
was one of the ringleaders of the Arab terrorist move-

ment. However, when the chips were down, he turned out to be a very competent fighter against the Vichy French.

Describing his men's appearance on their nightly patrols into enemy territory, Dayan relates that they carried revolvers, hand-grenades, first-aid equipment, food, water-flasks and flash-lamps. They were supposed to look like Arabs and in fact wore Arab head-dress, but that was as far as the resemblance went! For the rest they wore khaki and rubber boots, with puttees tied securely around their ankles. As Arabs their external appearance was hardly convincing, but even worse was the fact that with the exception of their guide, only one of the men spoke Arabic.

The night of Saturday, June 8, was clear and bright, the sky above Hanita dotted with twinkling stars. In the kibbutz's dining room Australian troops ate together with Dayan's men. The invasion was about to begin.

Two hours later the Jewish fighters were on the other side of the border. 'Well,' Dayan joked, 'we've invaded. Now we can go back home.' But they continued on their way, skirting villages so as not to arouse their sleeping inhabitants. It was tough going through the mountains. In the report Dayan submitted after the operation, he also described in vivid detail the beautiful scenery through which they passed. He told poetically of how, when dawn came and the men were marching along the western ledge of the Lebanese Mountains, they saw the first rays of the sun strike the Mediterranean.

The invading force with which Dayan operated was commanded by Captain Henry Gowling. It was split into two sections: one set out for the Beirut–Haifa highway and the other for the Iskanderun Bridge. Dayan accompanied the latter. The bridge was located about twelve miles from the frontier and, when they came within sight of it, the Australian captain decided that he, the Arab guide and Dayan would get near it and see whether there were any French troops on guard. The Australian was an expert on explosives and sabotage operations. He warned Dayan not to remove his finger from the trigger as he followed the guide for fear the Arab might betray them.

The bridge was unguarded. The French had blown up the road further south, closer to the Palestine border, and the bridge was therefore left intact. Dayan's men decided to cut the French telephone lines. But the men saw no signs of the main invading force arriving and they began to get bored with lack of action. They decided to make for the police station not far from the Iskanderun Bridge. Dayan suggested to Gowling that they capture the building from the French and leave a guard behind to secure the bridge. The captain agreed and the men moved forward towards their objective, unaware of the fact that inside the police station a large French force was awaiting them. Dayan's men were in high spirits, laughing and joking as though they were on a school outing. It was only when they were within about two hundred yards of their objective that they noticed there was a considerable movement of khaki-clad men inside. Their suspicions were aroused but it was too late. The French opened fire, and Dayan's men dived for cover in a nearby grove. Between them the Jewish fighters had, apart from their revolvers, five sub-machine guns, two rifles, and two hand-grenades. Under withering fire from the French defenders, the men edged forward from the depths of the grove towards the stone wall surrounding the police building.

A machine-gun was trained directly upon the attackers, and the situation became critical. Dayan pulled the pin from one of his hand-grenades and lobbed it straight at the machine-gun, which was firing from the open balcony of the building, a distance of almost twenty yards. The machine-gun was silenced, and ten men rushed forward to the attack, shooting at the windows and doors with whatever they had. Moshe threw his second grenade into the heart of the building. The attack was so fast and furious that it overwhelmed the French defenders. Complete surrender came within minutes.

There were eight fully armed Frenchmen inside the building and two others unarmed, in addition to several wounded men lying on the floor. The Haganah party disarmed their prisoners and locked them in a room, while Moshe Dayan took charge of the machine-gun, the like of which he had never seen before. They carried the gun to the roof and decided to hold on to the police station until the Australian invasion force arrived. In the adjacent grove they discovered more French armaments and supplies, including a mortar, about sixty horses, communications equipment and a motor cycle and sidecar. From the roof of the building they could see other large groups of French troops dug in over the surrounding countryside. The French began to snipe at the men on the roof, and Dayan found that there were no more ammunition belts for his machine-gun. Bullets were removed from rifles and an ammunition belt was thus filled. Dayan was able to return the French fire. But there was no way of taking cover on the roof and he stood fully exposed to the snipers' bullets. As he raised his field-glasses to his eyes in search of the enemy snipers, a bullet hit the left lens, smashing his eye.

Zalman Mart was downstairs when the battle began, guarding the prisoners. When he heard what had happened to Dayan, he dashed upstairs to give first aid. It was a frightening sight. Dayan was still conscious, but his left eye was gone, leaving only a blood-filled socket. Mart asked Moshe how he felt. 'Not bad,' was the reply. 'If I can get to hospital within three hours I'll certainly live.' Dayan's voice was calm and his tone level. Mart and an Australian soldier wrapped him in a blanket and lowered him from the roof. He was placed on the floor of one of the building's two rooms. Bullets crashed through the windows and whistled above his head, but for all his pain and discomfort, Dayan appeared to be unmoved. He ordered his men to return to their positions and keep the French busy instead of bothering with him. 'He certainly behaved like a hero,' Zalman Mart recalls twenty-six years later, 'I shall never forget the courage he displayed at that time.'

When the main Australian force arrived from Palestine, the French realised their situation was hopeless and abandoned the fight. Only then were Dayan and a dead Australian soldier loaded on a truck carrying booty and taken back to Haifa. They reached there, after a terrible journey over difficult terrain, about eighteen hours after Dayan had been wounded. Moshe neither ate nor drank a thing during all that time. Nor did he bother any of his men or ask for aid or comfort. In Haifa he was immediately given medical care at the Hadassah Hospital, but his left eye remained in the Lebanon.

The capture of Syria and the Lebanon served to relieve the immediate danger facing the British forces in the Middle East. Until that summer the threat had been serious, for with the Vichy forces were units of the German and Italian air forces, while in spring, 1941, pro-Nazi elements under Rashid Ali had gained control of Iraq. But by summer's end, Rashid Ali had been overthrown, and British and Soviet forces, now allied after Hitler's invasion of Russia, had also occupied Iran. Nevertheless, as Hitler's hordes advanced eastwards and southwards on the Russo-Ukrainian fronts there were realistic fears of a possible German push through the Caucasus and Turkey into Iraq to capture the oilfields there.

In 1941, British Headquarters in the Middle East approached the Jewish Agency with a suggestion that a network of radio stations be set up in Palestine to be used for espionage purposes on behalf of the British in the event of a German invasion of the country.

Moshe Dayan had been released from hospital only a few weeks previously, wearing a black patch over the socket of his left eye. After the Syrian and Lebanese operations, the commando units which had participated became the nucleus of a new striking force known as the 'Palmach', (short for Plugot Machatz, or Shock Platoons), the formation of which had been decided upon on May 18, 1941. The Palmach was a permanent mobilised military group headed by Yitzhak Sadeh and financed by the British through the Jewish Agency. The British Army provided instruction for the force in

43

sabotage methods and the use of modern and sophisticated arms. Eventually the British withdrew their
financial support and the Palmach became an independent force. Its units were housed in kibbutzim where,
for three weeks of each month, they worked and helped
in the running of the communal settlements, which
suffered from a shortage of labour. In return, they were
provided with board and lodging and other necessities
for the whole month. The remaining week was devoted
to intensive military training. The Palmach, one of the
leaders of which was Yigal Allon, emerged as an efficient
fighting force which later undertook special tasks in the
Jewish struggle for independence. It operated against the
Mandatory Government, it brought immigrants into the
country illegally and finally it spearheaded Jewish
military action in the 1948 War of Independence.

Dayan did not rejoin the new force after his recovery
from his injuries. As a member of a moshav, he could not
agree that he be obliged to spend his time on a kibbutz,
while his father needed help to run his farm. He did not
want to give a kibbutz three weeks of work a month, at
the height of the agricultural season, for the sake of one
week's training. He was prepared to offer payment for
his one week's living expenses under military training, so
that during the rest of the month he would be free to
work on his father's farm at Nahalal.

It was because of this sort of dispute that the Palmach
became the kibbutz army, and very few of its members
originated from the towns or the villages. The High
Command of the Palmach even acquired certain political
leanings which did not conform with the views of the
heads of the Jewish Agency or of the Haganah. None-

theless, these differing political opinions never at any time caused a breach of discipline. Later, however, after the War of Independence, the Palmach became a centre of controversy, with the then Prime Minister and Minister of Defence, David Ben-Gurion, categorically opposing its continued existence as a separate military entity. The upshot was the disbanding of the Palmach. Ben Gurion's attitude resulted in a deterioration in the relations between himself and the Left-wing labour circles under whose auspices the Palmach had functioned and many of whose leaders had been Palmach officers, including such men as Yigal Allon, Moshe Carmel and Israel Galili. These men became political opponents of David Ben-Gurion and Moshe Dayan.

During the latter part of 1941, Dayan lived in Jerusalem with his wife and daughter. He was there to receive the medical treatment he required for his eye injury. While in Jerusalem, he was asked by Haganah headquarters and the Political Department of the Jewish Agency to undertake a special security mission. This, as explained to him by Moshe Shertok, head of the department (later, as Moshe Sharett, to be Israel's first Foreign Minister) was to organise the network of radio stations which were to serve as espionage agencies for the British in the event of a German occupation of Palestine.

The Palmach and Haganah headquarters had already drawn up plans to become effective in such an eventuality. They provided for guerrilla warfare against the Germans and even for the transformation of Haifa into a Jewish fortress, which would have become a second Massada, defended as valiantly and perhaps even as tragically as the first was against the Romans.

The British wanted a limited radio network. On August 15, 1941, Dayan suggested establishing a larger network which would cover the entire country. Each station would have a crew of four, one technician and three agents, who would supply information on German military movements. This was the project known as the 'Palestine Scheme', except in Haganah circles where it was referred to as 'Moshe Dayan's Private Network'. Special courses in the use of radio equipment were started under Dayan's direction, in the first of which twenty-three men participated. A radio station was set up in the Dayans' temporary residence in Katamon, a suburb of Jerusalem, where Ruth, with two-and-a-half-year-old Yael at her side, operated the equipment under the direction of two British intelligence agents. In the midst of these activities, Ruth gave birth to her second child, a son, Ehud.

But for Moshe, setting up the radio network was only one of the things to be done in preparation for a Nazi invasion. In October 1941, he suggested the formation of sabotage units. These would consist of Jews disguised as Arabs and Germans, who would stay and operate behind the German lines and in conjunction with the British Army. In view of the information which had reached Palestine from German-occupied areas of Europe, Dayan realised it would be extremely difficult for Jews to operate after such an invasion except in disguise.

The suggestion was not acted upon at the time, but later the British were in need of German-speaking combatants for sabotage operations behind the lines of Rommel's Afrika Korps in the Western Desert. They remembered Dayan's plan. In May 1942, the Palmach set up a 'German Department' under the command of two German-speaking officers, Shimon (Koch) Avidan and Israel Karmi, which undertook missions on behalf of the British Army behind enemy lines. At a later stage, towards the close of 1943, Dayan's plan was taken a step further when the British recognised the fighting ability of the Palestine Jews. Parachute units were formed and Palestinians who originated from countries in Nazi-occupied southern Europe were dropped there to help the Allied war effort. Among them were the Hungarian-born Hannah Senesz and the Italian-born Enzo Sereni, both of whom met their deaths at the hands of the Germans while engaged on such missions.

In 1942, when Sereni was serving as a Haganah emissary in Baghdad, Dayan got to know that a Jewish bus company had been asked to help transport Indian Army units to Iraq. Each of the Jewish bus drivers going with the convoy took a relief driver along, and Dayan managed to have himself chosen as one of these. After a long and exhausting journey, the convoy arrived at its destination, a British Army camp outside Baghdad. However, the Jews were forbidden to enter the city with their vehicles for fear that they might be attacked by Arab troublemakers. They all, including Dayan, spent the night at the camp. The next morning he noticed crowds of ragged Arab labourers working on the canal leading into the city. As he himself later recounted, he disguised himself in a long Arab shirt and joined a group of labourers making their way into Baghdad. Once there, he found the hotel where Sereni was staying and asked to see him. But the janitor, seeing this miserably dressed,

47

one-eyed individual, tried to chase him away, and only
after much argument was Dayan able to prevail upon
him to let Sereni know about his strange visitor. Sereni
took Dayan up to his room, dressed him in a decent suit
and took him on a sight-seeing tour of the Iraqi capital.
The next day Dayan returned to his bus driver companions and left with them for Palestine.

The Germans never managed to get anywhere near
the borders of Palestine, either via the Caucasus or via
the Western Desert. The espionage units which Dayan
had organised remained unemployed and the men
complained of their lack of activity. At that time many
young Palestine Jews joined the ranks of the Palmach,
while others volunteered for the British Army in response
to an appeal by the heads of the Jewish Agency. This was
to be followed in 1944 by the formation of the Jewish
Brigade, consisting of Palestinian volunteers. One of
those who joined the Brigade was Zohar Dayan, Moshe's
younger brother, who fought with the Allies in Italy.

Moshe Dayan, too, demanded action and when he
received no response, he tendered his resignation from
the network. He said that espionage and intelligence
work were all very interesting, but the main thing was to
plan and prepare actual combat operations. The Jewish
Agency leaders managed to persuade him to withdraw
his resignation. Dayan suddenly realised, it seems, that
what he was doing in organising the network and other
missions connected with it would have a great bearing
upon the development of the embryo Jewish army. At
that stage, when the Jewish population of Palestine
numbered about 600,000, its leaders were preparing for
the possibility of an armed struggle. There were now

40,000 men in the Haganah, of whom only 1,600, in the Palmach, were well trained. The arms at their disposal included some 10,000 rifles, less than 500 sub-machine guns, about 125 machine-guns and 4,000 revolvers. Some of the Haganah's best fighters went abroad to serve in the Jewish Brigade.

Meanwhile, Dayan carried on unobtrusively with his Haganah duties. He attended secret sessions of the 'Young Turks', the leaders of the Haganah and the Palmach but, with his highly individual outlook, he did not wield much influence among them. At a time when the feeling was widespread among Palestine Jews that national independence could only be won with the aid of outside allies, Dayan stuck to the view that basically the Jews must rely upon themselves. He did not share the belief, held by many, that Britain would impose a settlement corresponding to the Jewish conception of the National Home promised in the Balfour Declaration. Likewise, he rejected the idea, advanced by the Leftists who were prominent in the Haganah and other national institutions, that there was something to be gained by association with the Communist world. Instead, Dayan insisted on the need to build up the Jews' own military and economic strength, while seeking direct negotiations with the Palestine Arabs. It was an attitude he was to maintain, with due regard to changing circumstances, throughout his career.

# 3

## Bold Strokes in the War of Independence

As the second world war drew to an end, the Jewish population of Palestine was plunged into grief and desolation. The first survivors from Europe arrived in the country with barely credible tales of the fate which had overtaken the once flourishing Jewish communities of the Continent. Only too quickly was the final terrible truth fully known. There was hardly a Jewish family in Palestine which had not lost relatives or friends in the Nazi holocaust. To some the disaster spelt the end of the Zionist dream, the dashing of all hopes for the establishment of a Jewish State. But this view was not shared by the leaders of the Jewish community. Amongst them the opinion gained ground that the moment was riper than ever before for the fulfilment of Zionist aspirations. The twin facts of the considerable contribution made by the Jews of Palestine to the war effort against the Nazis and of the enormous losses and suffering inflicted upon European Jewry must, it was believed, bring the nations of the world to recognise the Jews' right to a State of their own. There were also grounds for assuming that Britain would be obliged to abandon her anti-Zionist White Paper policy of 1939 which stripped the Jews of many of their rights in Palestine.

The Biltmore Programme, adopted by Zionist leaders at their conference held in May, 1942, at the Biltmore

Hotel in New York, had lost most of its relevance. This programme called for the immediate transfer of two million Jewish refugees from Europe to Palestine for the express purpose of creating a Jewish majority there. The Biltmore Programme was the cause of heated debate among Zionist leaders and created a gulf in the relations between the late Dr Chaim Weizmann, later to become first President of Israel, and David Ben-Gurion, when the latter chose to give the widest possible interpretation to the decisions taken at the conference. But, by the time the war ended, these decisions had become practically meaningless. There were no longer two million Jewish refugees left alive to transfer from Europe to Palestine.

Britain, for her part, caused the Jews of Palestine the deepest feelings of disillusion when the British Labour Party came to power in 1945. The party's totally unexpected decision to pursue the notorious White Paper policy, in total, and even cynical, disregard of the suffering of the Jewish survivors living in camps in Germany, Austria and Italy, aroused a wave of bitter hatred against Britain. Relations between the Mandatory Government of Palestine and the leaders of the Jewish community became extremely tense. The Jewish Agency refused to acquiesce in the British policy of restricting immigration and started organising the illegal transfer to Palestine of thousands of Jews from the Displaced Persons' camps in Europe. Many of them were caught by the British and interned in Cyprus. A leading role in this illegal immigration was played by the Palmach.

There were two other Jewish underground bodies which carried opposition to British policy a step further. Both were offshoots of the New Zionist (or Revisionist)

51

Organisation, founded before the war by Zeev Jabotinsky in protest against the hesitancy of orthodox Zionists
in defining their aim as the establishment of a fully
fledged Jewish State. Jabotinsky, a flamboyant character
who had fought for the British in the First World War,
was briefly imprisoned by them in 1920 for organising
armed Jewish self-defence against Arab rioters in
Jerusalem. He was detained in the same gloomy Fortress
of Acre where Dayan and his forty-two companions were
sent twenty years later. In the thirties Jabotinsky called for
the speedy evacuation of European Jewry to Palestine,
and his movement's military arm, the *Irgun Tzvai Leumi*
(National Military Organisation) was prepared to use
force to attain that goal. On the outbreak of war against
Germany, however, the Irgun decided temporarily to
sink its differences with the British. The Irgun's commander, David Raziel, was, in fact, killed in 1941 while on a
mission for the British against pro-Nazi forces which had
surrounded the British base at Habbaniya, in Iraq.

But a number of Irgun members, rejecting any idea
of co-operation with Britain, broke away to form a new
group, called the *Lohmei Herut Israel* (Fighters for the
Freedom of Israel) or Lehi for short. This group, known
to the British as the Stern Gang, was headed by Avraham
Stern, who was shot dead by British police in 1942 while
trying to escape arrest. To his followers he became a
martyr and a myth. Although Lehi stemmed from the
same root as the Irgun, the two groups held widely
divergent political opinions. The Irgun took as its objective the re-creation of a Jewish State within its historic
boundaries, on both sides of the River Jordan. Lehi, on
the other hand, consisted of extremists who ranged in

outlook from orthodox religious to pro-Communist.

With the end of the war, both the Irgun and Lehi embarked upon a campaign of terror against the British. Their activities were at first a grave source of embarrassment to the Jewish Agency. An investigation into the two terrorist groups was carried out by the Haganah in 1944, and there ensued a period during which it cooperated with the British police against them.

Moshe Dayan was not to be found among the organisers of illegal immigration at that time, nor was he active with the combat units of the Palmach, even though he had been one of the founders of the force. Occasionally he could be seen going in or out of the old building which housed the Executive Committee of the Histadrut in Tel Aviv, and where Haganah Headquarters were also located. Sometimes he would be on night patrol in the plains near Nahalal or the hills of Galilee. Then he would be in the company of Jews who looked remarkably like Arabs. At one stage he tried to remove the obstacles separating the underground organisations, so as to bring them together for joint action. Through his intervention, contact was made between Haganah Headquarters and the leaders of Lehi, for it was specifically the latter group which interested Dayan. He considered its members to be daring and courageous fighters whose talents and energies it would be worth while directing into better and more effective channels.

He was to hold the same opinion several years later when, in 1948, he was given command of an assault unit and told to select his own men from the ranks of the Israeli forces. He chose them carefully from the crack units of the Haganah, the Palmach and Lehi.

Except on rare occasions, Dayan was never seen with the top brass of the Haganah. This was perhaps due to his having held himself aloof from political activities, for there was a direct connection in those days between one's political views and activities and the rank one held in the Palmach or Haganah hierarchy. Dayan was not a kibbutz member, and did not see eye to eye with the Left-wing group which ran the Palmach. Nor did he show any interest in being active in Mapai, even though he belonged to the party and to a moshav which was outspokenly pro-Mapai. Thus it was that he lost his position in leadership and had to make way for men who had served during the war as officers in the British Army.

But Dayan did carry out certain special missions for the Haganah in matters of day-to-day security, in intelligence and, above all, in preparing for the future. It was generally accepted that the use of force against the Arabs could not be avoided, and that it might as a last resort have to be used against the British in order to assure the establishment of the Jewish State. Between 1945 and 1946, while he was serving with the permanent staff of the Haganah, he often stayed in a small room in a Tel Aviv Hotel, but his home remained in Nahalal. There, in 1943, he had purchased his own farm from a member-farmer who decided to leave the village. On it he kept cows and chickens, working and managing the farm by himself. At the end of the war Ruth had given birth to their third and last child, a son, whom they named Assaf.

The pace of violence quickened in Palestine, with both Jews and Arabs preparing for the coming showdown. The British finally referred the question to the United

Nations which, in November, 1947, voted in favour of the partition of the country into a Jewish and an Arab State, politically independent but linked together economically, with Jerusalem as an international enclave. The Arab countries rejected the plan. Several weeks before the final British departure, fixed for May 15, 1948, widespread fighting broke out, with British troops watching from the sidelines. In this twilight period, between peace and full-scale war, Moshe Dayan re-emerged as a Haganah trouble-shooter, being sent to deal with flare-ups in various sectors.

In April the Dayan family suffered a grievous loss. Moshe's younger brother, Zohar, was killed in an armed encounter with Druse tribesmen near the settlements of Usha and Ramat Yohanan, north of Haifa. This was before the Druses decided to join the Jewish side in the Palestine conflict. The death of his brother, whom he loved dearly, was a bitter blow for Moshe, but in those desperate days there was little time for mourning. On April 22 the Haganah took control of Haifa, and Dayan was dispatched post-haste to the city by Haganah Headquarters to prevent any plundering of abandoned British Army stores there, which were vital for the Jewish defence effort.

In another action which took place during the British withdrawal, the Arab Legion of King Abdullah of Transjordan (later Jordan), aided by thousands of Palestinian Arab irregulars, sacked Kfar Etzion and three other Jewish settlements in the Judean Hills between Bethlehem and Hebron. This was probably the greatest single reverse suffered by the Jews in the whole of the 1948 fighting. The whole Etzion Block fell to the

Legion. Many of the surrendering Jews were then mercilessly massacred by local Arabs, before the rest were taken prisoner.

On Friday afternoon, May 14, the eve of the Sabbath, an historic assembly was convoked in the building of the Tel Aviv Jewish Museum, where the Jewish leaders proclaimed the establishment of the State of Israel and the formation of a provisional Government, with David Ben-Gurion as Prime Minister and Defence Minister. At the same time the armies of seven Arab countries, Egypt, Syria, Transjordan, the Lebanon, Iraq, Saudi Arabia and the Yemen, announced their intention of invading Palestine the following day, when the British Mandate ended, to wage a Jihad (holy war) against the Jews. But already the Arab Legion had moved over to the West Bank of the Jordan, while units of the Egyptian Army had entered southern Palestine. In the north, Syrian infantry and armour were pouring down from the Golan Heights towards the Jewish settlements of the Jordan Valley. Their first objective was Degania, where Dayan was born thirty-three years before.

Two days after the Declaration of Statehood, the Syrian forces succeeded in capturing the police station at Zemach, which was an important strategic position in the area. The Syrians attempted to storm Degania, but they were held by the kibbutzniks, who fought back courageously, throwing Molotov cocktails at the advancing tanks and setting them ablaze. The Syrians kept up relentless pressure, using vastly superior armament, and two other Jewish settlements in the area, Massada and Sha'ar Hagolan, had to be abandoned by their defenders.

The inhabitants of Degania and the neighbouring

settlements among whom were leading personalities in the Jewish Agency, the labour movement and the Haganah, sent a desperate appeal to Ben-Gurion demanding urgent help and warning that they might have to abandon their homes if it was not forthcoming.

The assistance the General Staff could spare was negligible, although on several occasions during the battle against the Syrian attackers light aircraft of Israel's tiny Air Force, had been in operation for the very first time. Headquarters sent what it could to the settlements in the Jordan Valley. The aid consisted of several pieces of First World War French artillery! Moshe Dayan was in charge of building up a second line of defence. On May 20, five days after the Syrians had penetrated the Jordan Valley, the Israelis recaptured the Zemach police station, repulsed Syrian attacks on Degania and forced the Syrian Army to withdraw from the Jordan Valley.

One of Dayan's exploits during this campaign is related by an old school friend of his, Avinoam Slutzky, who took part in the defence of Degania. After they had been driven from the immediate area, the Syrians installed field guns on the hill of Tel el Kasr, near the south-eastern tip of the Sea of Galilee. From here they continued to bombard the Jordan Valley settlements, out of range of any artillery the Israelis had at the time. Dayan got together a group of 14 volunteers, mostly from the Nahalal district, including Slutzky, and set out for a raid on the Syrian position. They rowed across the Sea of Galilee in two small boats and moored them on the eastern shore, just south of the kibbutz of Ein Gev. Then they made their way towards Tel el Kasr, creeping the

57

last few dozen yards under cover of darkness. They climbed the hill and managed to plant enough explosive charges to wreck the battery. The noise of the explosion spread panic among the nearby Syrian troops, who thought they had been attacked by a strong Israeli force and retreated to positions further east. This version of events was later confirmed by members of Ein Gev who had picked up radio messages from the Syrians at Tel el Kasr telling their headquarters that they could not hold out. Meanwhile the 14 Israelis returned safely to their base. Subsequently Tel el Kasr became the site of a Jewish kibbutz, Tel Katzir (now renamed Beit Katzir).

On June 11, 1948, a temporary one month truce was arranged by the United Nations Mediator, Count Bernadotte. The truce enabled the Israeli forces to consolidate the transformation they had undergone in battle from an underground organisation into a regular army. This army now had time to integrate a number of mechanised units into its infantry brigades and to prepare for a counter offensive.

During the truce United Nations observers maintained a strict watch to ensure that the combatants should not increase their strength by bringing in reinforcements from outside. But a ship called the *Altalena*, with a cargo of munitions for Israel, had already set sail before the truce came into effect. Both vessel and cargo had been purchased by Irgun supporters and sympathisers in Europe and the United States. Agreement had already been reached between the Irgun High Command and the Israeli Government that the Irgun should be disbanded and its men mobilised into the regular forces of the Israeli Army. The Irgun now approached Ben-

Gurion, as Minister of Defence, and asked for Government guidance as to what was to be done with the *Altalena* and its cargo. Ben-Gurion referred the matter to his deputy, Israel Galili, who had been one of the heads of the Haganah and Palmach. In discussions with the Commander-in-Chief of the Irgun, Menahem Begin, Galili agreed that the cargo should be off-loaded near Kfar Vitkin between Haifa and Tel Aviv.

The mutual distrust which existed between the leaders of the Irgun and the Haganah apparently permeated their discussions on the *Altalena* and its cargo. On June 22, when the vessel reached the coast, the Irgun asked the Government to off-load the cargo but added a condition that twenty per cent of the arms be transferred to Irgun units operating in Jerusalem. The Government rejected the condition and ordered the Army to prevent the ship unloading at Kfar Vitkin. The Alexandroni Brigade, under the command of Brigadier Dan Even, surrounded the area to carry out the order. Simultaneously, Irgun units converged upon Kfar Vitkin, among them many soldiers who had left their units to aid in off-loading their ship.

A tense and dangerous situation was rapidly developing. Haganah Headquarters dispatched its trouble-shooter, Moshe Dayan, with a unit of commando troops to keep the situation under control but, before he reached the scene, the *Altalena* raised anchor and sailed off in the direction of Tel Aviv. There, on the sandy beach opposite Palmach Headquarters in the Red House, and in full view of the foreign Press corps staying at the Ritz Hotel, the *Altalena* ran itself aground the following day, June 23.

Her first intention was to unload straight on to the Herbert Samuel Quay which skirted the sea-shore. As a background to the drama, accusations were flying back and forth, with the Irgun High Command claiming the Government had purposely led them into a trap, while the Government accused the Irgun of trying to organise a military coup.

Meanwhile all attention was focused on the sea-shore as the Irgun commander on board the *Altalena* and the Army officers ashore shouted at each other through megaphones. Suddenly, in the midst of the parley, a burst of gunfire came from the direction of Palmach Headquarters. A shell struck the vessel which caught fire. Six *Altalena* volunteers were killed, and dozens wounded. One of the dead was Abraham Stavsky, one of the heads of the Irgun. Most of the weapons and ammunition on board the stricken vessel were lost in the blaze, and the heavy pall of smoke which blackened the skies above Tel Aviv carried an implicit threat of civil war. It was Menahem Begin who saved the situation. In an impassioned speech to the public, broadcast over the Irgun's clandestine radio station, he ordered his men to return to their units in the Army and prepare themselves for the fight against the Arab invaders. Civil war was prevented, but bitterness over the loss of the *Altalena* was to dominate Begin's mind for the next nineteen years. He referred to the incident time and time again and from every public platform on which he spoke.

Some days after the *Altalena* incident, Moshe Dayan and another senior officer flew to the United States to represent the Israeli Government at the funeral of

Colonel David Marcus at West Point. Colonel Marcus, an American volunteer, had commanded the Israeli forces in the Jerusalem Corridor, and had been shot in error by a sentry on June 11 following the start of the first truce.

While in the United States Dayan declared that the Israeli Army could conquer the whole of Palestine within six to eight weeks. On returning home, he was ordered to report to Brigadier-General Yitzhak Sadeh, who commanded a new armoured brigade formed during the truce.

As part of a general plan of campaign which bore the code name 'Operation Danny', under the command of Brigadier-General Yigal Allon, a large Israeli force, consisting of five infantry brigades and Sadeh's armoured brigade, was to eradicate the bulge formed by the Arab towns of Lydda and Ramleh situated less than ten miles from Tel Aviv. This was one of the major offensive operations embarked upon by the Jewish army when fighting recommenced after the ending of the first truce. By the time a second truce came into effect, on July 18, they had succeeded in wiping out the forces threatening Tel Aviv, widening the corridor to Jerusalem and loosening the Egyptian stranglehold on the Jewish settlements in the Negev.

Sadeh set great hopes upon the bold methods employed by Moshe Dayan, whom he knew well from the Hanita days, and gave the young officer a free hand in selecting the men he wanted for the commando unit he was forming. Dayan chose dozens of the soldiers he thought most suitable from Sadeh's own brigade and from other units but then went in search of ex-Lehi men.

61

Within a few days a new unit made its appearance: the 89th (Commando) Battalion of Moshe Dayan.

The tactics followed by Israeli commanders during the first stage of the War of Independence had been essentially static. Their forces remained in defence positions and kept strictly to the axis of movement (lines of advance and retreat) mapped out for them. The commanders favoured the system of first softening-up the target and then deploying their forces, while still a considerable distance from it, in preparation for the advance. But as the war developed, these defensive tactics proved to be a hindrance. True, they reduced casualties, but they also lacked momentum and prevented incisive victories over the enemy. A more dynamic approach was needed.

Within the Lydda-Ramleh bulge was a civilian population of 100,000 Arabs and thousands of troops, including irregulars as well as units of the Arab Legion. The Arab forces were attempting to link up with the Egyptian Army at Ashdod and thus cut Tel Aviv off from the southern part of the country. To defeat the Arab plans, the Israeli Supreme Command deployed its troops in a pincer movement. The intention was to sever the bulge from the Arab forces holding the Latrun area. Sadeh's armoured brigade was given the task of effecting a breakthrough in depth into enemy-held territory. Dayan's battalion, as part of Sadeh's brigade, was to storm the villages and fortified positions north-east of the bulge and thus gain commanding positions overlooking Lydda and the nearby international airport.

Dayan's initiative and enterprise in successfully capturing such villages and positions as Beit Naballah and Dir Taarif, did not gain any immediate recognition from the other officers who took part in 'Operation Danny'. But an enemy officer, Colonel Abdullah el Tel, of the Arab Legion, wrote in his memoirs of the Palestine War that in his opinion the moment of decision in the struggle between Israel and Jordan came when the fortified positions north-east of Lydda and Ramleh fell to the Israeli Army. Before the war was over Dayan and el Tel were to have a good deal to do with each other.

The British Commander of the Arab Legion, Brigadier Sir John Glubb, or Glubb Pasha as he was known to the Arabs, concurred with el Tel in considering the positions captured by Dayan as of vital importance in the battle for Lydda and Ramleh and in securing the road from Tel Aviv to Jerusalem. El Tel wrote that the fall of Lydda and Ramleh marked the end of Arab threats to Tel Aviv; it gave the Jews control of the international airport at Lydda; it provided them with a railway network throughout the country; it assured them of freedom of movement between Tel Aviv and Jerusalem; and it opened the way south by exposing the right flank of the Egyptian Army which had reached Ashdod, only twenty-three miles from Tel Aviv. It also enabled the Jews to release large numbers of troops to increase their pressure on the Jerusalem front.

The first temporary truce came to an end on July 9, following the rejection by the Arabs of Count Bernadotte's extension, which Israel had accepted. Three days later Dayan's battalion had occupied the villages to the north-east of the bulge, thus relieving a small Israeli force which had been cut off at the Ben Shemen Jewish Agricultural School.

The occupation of Dir Taarif and its surrounding fortified positions, as well as of the military camp at Beit Naballah, which the British had handed over to the Arab Legion, was completed during the morning of July 12, after a battle lasting thirty hours. The Arab Legion had withdrawn, leaving behind a tank which had overturned and lay on its side. Dayan's men had taken cover at the foot of a hill and were gazing covetously at the disabled tank. They could do with at least one tank, armed with a cannon, and this one, which the British had supplied to the Arab Legion, had a two-pounder mounted on it. That tank was a great temptation, for their mobile equipment consisted only of twelve jeeps, armed with machine-guns, and several tracked armoured cars. The Legionnaires were keeping a sharp eye on the Israelis to prevent them getting near the tank. But Dayan's men wanted the tank too desperately to be thwarted. They crawled to the tank, tied a rope to it and, with the help of a tractor hidden from the Arab Legionnaires, dragged it into camp under a hail of Arab bullets. Dayan inspected the tank and was delighted with the cannon. He ordered one of the men to fire at a target at a range of 500 yards. The result was a direct hit and one olive tree wiped out. The soldier was immediately appointed tank-gunner by Dayan and the vehicle dubbed 'The Terrible Tiger'. Someone scrawled the words 'Nahalal-Amman Express' on its side, and on the gun barrel 'Straight to the Point'.

When the boys had finished amusing themselves with their new toy, they looked westwards and saw the houses of Lydda and the town's green orchards spread out as though on the open palm of a hand, waiting to be taken.

On appointment as Chief of Staff, 7th December 1953

Receiving the Legion of Honour from General Guillaume, Paris 1954

Dayan with Lavon in 1954. Peres is between them (at back)

Dayan decided that this was as good a moment as any other for an attack on the town, particularly while its north-east flank was exposed. The defenders would not expect an attack from that direction. He did not wait for orders from operational headquarters but got his battalion ready for a quick, powerful drive, with the 'Terrible Tiger' leading the way.

The men were exhausted from the battles they had fought during the past two days, but the news that they were to attack Lydda gave them new energy. They had suffered casualties in the recent fighting, but those two days had moulded them into a co-ordinated force, and Dayan knew he could rely upon their fighting spirit. He was taking an enormous responsibility in deciding to attack but he ordered the battalion to advance; the die was cast. The 'Terrible Tiger' led the column, with Dayan riding behind in the first armoured car. A few of the jeeps had driven ahead of the column as scouts.

At the entrance to Lydda the Israelis encountered a large enemy force and powerful fire raked them from all sides. 'Storm through!' Dayan ordered over his walkie-talkie, 'Beat them! Smash them!' He ordered the column to fan out, leaving the 'Tiger' to overwhelm the first-line defences.

'Carry on! Move!' was his next command. 'No stopping for anything. The column must not stop under any circumstances.' The column continued its assault and reached the centre of town. The 'Terrible Tiger' roared up and down the main streets, while the jeeps set off for the adjoining town of Ramleh. The inhabitants of the two towns were stupefied. They had no idea of what was happening. The local Arab Legion commander came out of his headquarters in the Lydda police fortress and, seeing the tank, which he recognised, he waved at it and cheered, thinking it to be the vanguard of reinforcements for his troops! When two Israeli jeeps accelerated towards him, he vanished instantly inside the fortress and locked the gates behind him.

Despite the heavy fire poured on them through the embrasures the Israelis attacked the fortress. Dayan arrived in front of the building in his armoured car. He ordered his main force to make for Ramleh, leaving only a squad of troops to keep the Legionnaires pinned down inside their fortress.

Four years later, in 1952, when he was taking an advanced course at the Military College at Earlston Park, England, Dayan was to meet Major Adib el Kassem of the Arab Legion. During a friendly discussion, the Jordanian officer told Dayan of his experiences in the 1948 War and of the heroic attack by a Jewish commando force, which had stormed its way into Lydda and Ramleh. The Arab Legion commander, entrenched inside the Lydda police fortress, had tried to keep the Israelis at bay but could not because of their ferocious fire-power. He had escaped with his men towards Latrun. El Kassem did not know he was speaking to the man who had led the attack. He was full of praise for the courage of the Israeli troops who had attacked the two Arab towns and spread panic among the demoralised inhabitants.

When he reached the centre of Ramleh, which straddles the highway from the coast to Jerusalem, Dayan ordered an about-turn and roared back to his base camp. On the way back through the towns he again ordered his men to sweep the streets with concentrated bursts of gunfire. As he neared camp next to the Jewish village of Ben Shemen, he was met by a murderous rain of fire coming from the direction of Lydda. The Arab troops there had managed to recover and reorganise after their initial rout. Dayan's battalion suffered casualties but overwhelmed the remaining defences in both Lydda and Ramleh, this time aided by other Israeli units which had set out to capture the towns. The Arab population had had enough fighting and began to flee the towns in huge numbers. The Arab Legion disappeared in the direction of the Jordan, and the Arab irregular forces withdrew from the area. Dayan informed the Israeli infantry units now attacking the outskirts of Lydda that there was nothing to stop them walking straight into the town. Two infantry brigades entered Lydda and mopped up the remnants of the stunned and routed Arab forces. Dayan drove back to his base. Fifty minutes had passed from the moment he burst into Lydda! Resting in the shade of two ancient olive trees, the 89th Battalion added up its losses: nine dead, sixteen wounded and most of its vehicles damaged.

The men asked for a breathing spell, but the next day, July 13, Dayan received new instructions from the High Command. Brigadier-General Yigal Yadin, Chief of Operations, wanted the battalion reorganised at once for an urgent mission on the southern front as part of Operation *Mavet Lapolesh* (Death to the Invader). The object of the operation was to break the Egyptian stranglehold on the Negev. Dayan begged for a respite for his exhausted troops but, despite the cogency of his arguments, the issue was decided by the personal intervention of

Ben-Gurion. The operation was urgent. Dayan returned to his base at Tel Litvinsky, a former British Army camp (which today houses a large hospital and is called Tel Hashomer). Ben-Gurion's orders rang in his ears. The Egyptian ring must be broken. It must be broken at all costs, even at the cost of the 89th Battalion. When the battle was finished another battalion could be formed, but the vital issue was the road to the Negev. It must be opened.

There was no time to spare. Five days had passed since the end of the truce, and a new resolution for the imposition of another truce was before the United Nations. Several military victories gained during these first five days had given the Israelis encouragement, and it was important to improve their positions before they were forced to accept the new cease-fire. The Egyptians had built fortified positions along the east-west road leading from Beit Guvrin via Faluja to Ashkelon. To break the Egyptian blockade it was essential to capture the Arab village of Caratia and this, therefore, was the most important objective of Operation *Mavet Lapolesh*. The job was given to the 89th (Commando) Battalion, which was henceforth attached to the Givati Brigade operating on the southern front.

At his Tel Litvinsky headquarters, Dayan inspected his troops and equipment. Those of his vehicles which were not out of action, needed a thorough overhaul. Manpower was seriously depleted; several of the battalion's officers and N.C.Os had been killed. He informed Yadin of his misgivings and once again the latter consulted Ben-Gurion. The 'Old Man', however, was adamant. Dayan's unit must join the attacking force

'even if this battle means a heavy blow to the battalion.'
However, Ben-Gurion agreed to give six more half-tracks
to the battalion, which now had twelve jeeps, eight half-
tracks, four tracked open armoured cars, two primitive
home-made armoured vehicles and the 'Terrible Tiger',
which was its heaviest piece of equipment. Those paltry
few armoured vehicles earned the unit the glorious title
of an 'armoured battalion'. But if it were really to be put
to the test, the battalion would have great difficulty in
standing up against even medium weight weapons.
Dayan assembled his men to hear a summing-up of their
Lydda-Ramleh exploit and a brief outline of the operation to come, against Caratia.

The following morning, July 14, the battalion set out
for the south. It made camp in an orange grove near the
Masmiya crossroads, thirty miles south of Tel Aviv and
less than thirteen miles north of the coming battle
arena.

Dayan was invited to Brigade Headquarters where he
was given the battle-plan which provided for a night-
time penetration by his battalion into Caratia. He was to
capture the village but would be given a platoon of
infantry to help in holding it. Dayan was not in favour
of a night attack because of the difficulty of negotiating
the area with armoured vehicles in the dark. But
Operation *Mavet Lapolesh* had already been set for the
night of July 17–18, and Dayan had to fit himself into
the overall plan.

The two following nights, reconnaissance patrols were
sent out to learn the lie of the land. On the third night, at
22.00 hours, the 89th (Commando) Battalion went into
action once again. It had hardly started off when the

69

leading armoured car was put out of action by a mine,
but the column kept going. Following the tactics used at
Lydda, the vehicles advanced in single file ready to fan
out the moment one of them was hit. Led by the 'Terrible
Tiger' they advanced to within about 170 yards of the
Egyptian fortified positions, moving in silence broken
only by the quiet purring of the engines. As soon as the
force was close enough to make full use of its fire-power,
Dayan gave the order 'Fire!' Every weapon was fired,
sending a withering fusillade in the direction of the
Egyptian positions, several of which were evacuated
immediately. But the Israelis were within range of enemy
artillery which opened up a fierce bombardment. The
soldier who was in charge of the cannon on the 'Terrible
Tiger', and had been since its capture from the Arab
Legion, raised his head above the turret to get a better
aim and was hit by a bullet which killed him immediately. Six other men were badly wounded, and several
suffered minor injuries.

Dayan's orders were followed explicitly. He had told
his troops: 'Nobody is to stop for anything or anybody.
No assistance is to be given by anyone until we reach the
wadi (dry river bed). Nobody is to stop except by command or in order to open fire. Until we get to the wadi
the order is advance, penetrate, move, move, move, all
the time . . .'

But when the force reached the wadi, it was found to
be the biggest obstacle to its advance on the village.
Dayan could see himself being bogged down at the wadi
and ordered the wounded to be attended to and removed
to a safe place. Reconnaissance patrols were sent out and
came back with Egyptian prisoners and Arab villagers.

Other patrols tried to find a point at which it would be easy to cross the wadi. Meanwhile, most of the men were busy shoring up its banks in preparation for the crossing. The battalion was in a miserable state. Many of the vehicles had been hit and could not be used. The men were dead tired. The desert wind dried and irritated their throats. Dayan himself was utterly exhausted and felt unable to take vital decisions while in such a condition. He ordered a young officer to take charge for an hour while he himself lay down on the ground, wrapped in an Arab keffia (head-cloth), and went to sleep. When he woke up it was 03.30 hours, and the men had managed to move most of the equipment across the wadi. All Dayan had to do was give the order to advance.

At 04.00 hours, just before dawn, he gave the signal for the attack on the village to begin. The men took on a new lease of life immediately they heard the command. Scouts were sent ahead, and after them went the 'Terrible Tiger'. The infantry platoon which was to occupy the village stood by to await results. By early morning, Dayan and his men were inside Caratia. The road to the Negev was not yet open, but the capture of Caratia created a crucial breach in the Egyptian positions.

Dayan's successes at Lydda and Caratia were no more spectacular than those of other commanders, but in the opinion of the High Command, and particularly that of Ben-Gurion, Dayan had proved himself outstanding by reason of his daring, initiative, decisiveness and tenacity in the face of all obstacles. Nevertheless, his cold-blooded order to advance regardless of casualties was considered unacceptable in the Israeli Defence Forces in those days.

71

The senior officers of the 1948 War are still not ready to praise Dayan for his actions then. They acknowledged his initiative and achievements in the Lydda and Caratia battles but showed no inclination to reward them by raising him to a position on the General Staff.

# 4

## Arabian Nights

THE DAY DAYAN's 89th (Commando) Battalion completed its capture of Caratia coincided with the inception of the second of the two truce agreements negotiated by Count Folke Bernadotte, the Swedish mediator appointed by the United Nations. Bernadotte had endeavoured to prevent the resumption of hostilities after the first truce agreement, but the Arabs objected to extending the truce beyond July 9. It was the Arabs who forced a continuance of the war until a second cease-fire, voted for by the Security Council, came into force on July 18. Those nine days of fighting, however, gave Israel several important advantages.

Nevertheless, the position in Jerusalem was still serious. The main highway from the city to the coastal plain remained blocked, and supplies for the beleaguered Jerusalem Jews could be transported only along a makeshift 'Burma Road', built while the battles raged. This by-passed the main highway and was out of range of the Arab Legion's guns.

Jerusalem was now split in two. The Old City was entirely in the hands of the Arabs, who also commanded the north-eastern heights overlooking the city, thus cutting off the Hebrew University and the Hadassah Hospital, both on Mount Scopus, from the Jewish sector. The Jews held the major part of the New City, including the Arab districts of Katamon, Talbieh and Abu Tor. The kibbutz at Ramat Rahel, opposite Bethlehem, now marked the front line, while the road from Jerusalem to Bethlehem was partly inside Israel's territory forcing the Arabs to build an alternative road.

For the first time in many generations, Jews were barred access to the Wailing Wall, the only relic of the ancient Temple. The Jewish inhabitants of the Old City were prisoners in Arab hands and nearly all the synagogues in the centuries-old Jewish Quarter of the Old City had been destroyed. For centuries Jews seeking solace in prayer had made their way to Rachel's Tomb, on the outskirts of Bethlehem, or to the Cave of Machpela in Hebron. Access to these shrines, too, was now denied to them.* Legend had it that within the Cave of Machpela lie the bones of the Patriarchs and Matriarchs, buried in couples: Abraham with Sarah; Isaac with Rebecca; Jacob with Leah. Some say that yet another couple lies buried there – Adam and Eve. The Jews of Jerusalem never have been quite sure whose bones are contained in the Cave, and when somebody jokingly told a Jew, whom he met fervently praying near the steps leading up to it, that in fact a Moslem sheikh was buried there, the Jerusalemite in all seriousness replied: 'Well, if an Arab is buried there, he has become a great *tzadik* (a righteous man) because the Jews have prayed at his graveside for so many years.'

* Publisher's note: A mosque covers the Cave of Machpela, and for several centuries Jews have been allowed to go no further than the seventh step leading up to the entrance to the building housing the tombs of the Patriarchs. It is only since the Six-Day War that Jews have been actually allowed to visit the tombs.

74

Shortly before the second cease-fire, a Jewish attempt to storm back into the Old City through the Zion Gate and regain control of the Jewish Quarter and the Wailing Wall was thwarted. However, in another sector of the Jerusalem front, Israeli soldiers succeeded in capturing the Arab village of Ein Karem together with the locality known as 'Miss Carey's' (Miss Carey was an eccentric Englishwoman who kept a private chapel on a hilltop overlooking Ein Karem). They also took the villages of Malachia and Tzoba as well as the fortified positions which controlled the western approaches to the city.

After the failure to retake the Old City, considerable criticism was levelled at the commander of the Jerusalem area, Brigadier-General David Shaltiel, an experienced officer of German birth. The then Israeli Chief of Operations, Yigal Yadin, was later to state that if Shaltiel had obeyed the General Staff's instructions and attacked the district of Sheikh Jarrah, in the northern part of Jerusalem, the Old City would have fallen into Israeli hands. Whatever the truth of that, it was decided to move Shaltiel from Jerusalem and appoint a new commander there. Ben-Gurion's choice for the post was young Moshe Dayan, and he was appointed over the heads of several senior officers who were due for promotion. On July 23, five days after his victory at Caratia, Dayan became Israeli commander in Jerusalem, with the rank of Lieutenant-Colonel.

Looking back, it now seems obvious that Ben-Gurion's choice was not based solely on the military aspects and requirements of the post. He foresaw the possibility of reaching an agreement with Abdullah, King of Trans-jordan. He was fully aware that an agreement with the country which shared with Israel the custodianship of the Holy City was of supreme importance. The political and military role played by Egypt under King Farouk in those days was of little consequence, and the Egyptian army had been hopelessly outfought by the Israelis. In fact the Government of Israel attached little importance to any of the Arab States except Transjordan, at least so far as immediate planning was concerned.

Several exploratory discussions had been held prior to the war between King Abdullah and Mrs Golda Meir, who later became Israel's second Foreign Minister. The purpose of these dramatic meetings was to prevent war between Transjordan and Israel, but it was evident the Jordanian Monarch would not sit on the sidelines if all the other Arab States invaded Israel. He, too, wanted to share in the hoped-for Arab victory. The successes the Arab Legion gained over the Israelis in the Etzion area, in Jerusalem and at Latrun only helped to strengthen the King's attitude. Yet there were signs indicating a change of heart in Amman, especially after the rout of the Egyptian forces in the south. Ben-Gurion wanted to be ready for whatever developments might emerge. The man he put in charge of the Jerusalem front, therefore, had to be someone who could act as a negotiator with King Abdullah but who also was capable of using force, if necessary.

Dayan was received at the entrance to his new head-quarters in Jerusalem by a very smart-looking officer who gave him a magnificent salute. In those days, saluting was hardly known in the Israeli Army, and Dayan, in any case, was certainly not the man to concern himself with the niceties of military etiquette. The officer introduced himself as the aide-de-camp to the commander, expecting a smile of appreciation from his new boss. Instead, Dayan looked at him with his one eye, replied laconically: 'You were – until this minute', and walked into the building.

When Dayan arrived in Jerusalem, the Jewish sector was at the mercy of Arab Legion snipers, shooting from their fortified positions along the massive walls of the Old City. After the second truce came into force, the Arab Legion, in conjunction with units of the Egyptian Army, stationed south of Jerusalem and at Bethlehem, tried to create a new *fait accompli* by overrunning Israeli forward positions. The Arabs succeeded in recapturing positions in Ein Karem and other strategic points which had been in Israeli hands.

Dayan replied to these breaches of the truce agreement with a heavy hand. In August, the Egyptians took possession of the former British High Commissioner's residence, which overlooks Jerusalem from the south. The building was now in no man's land and was used solely by the International Red Cross. Dayan sent a force with orders to clear the Egyptians out of the residence. The Arabs counter-attacked, and the Israelis, who had orders not to occupy the residence itself, captured the fortified positions around it in the Agricultural Training Farm and in the Arab College. These acquisitions constituted strong bargaining points for Dayan who offered the Arabs a cease-fire. The chief United Nations observer in the divided city, General Reilly, called a meeting of the three commanders – Israeli, Transjordanian and Egyptian – in order to arrange this cease-fire agreement. It was at that meeting that Dayan first made the acquaintance of Colonel Abdullah el Tel, the Arab Legion officer who was to become Military Governor of the Old City. He also met the commander of the Egyptian forces operating south of the city, Ahmed Awad el Aziz, who was killed the very next day in a road accident. After a number of meetings, the three sides signed a protocol establishing the boundaries of no man's land in Jerusalem.

The general truce agreement, which had been in force since July 18 was, however, not adhered to as it should have been. On the southern front, the Egyptians maintained their blockade of the road to the Negev and prevented the Israelis from sending supplies to their beleaguered settlements and armed forces there. This was a direct breach of the agreement, which provided for free passage through the Caratia sector, captured by Dayan and the 89th (Commando) Battalion, for six hours of each day. On one or two occasions Israeli forces endeavoured to break the Egyptian blockade, and on October 15 these incidents flared up into a renewal of the fighting on the southern front. This time the Israelis gained the advantage and followed it up across Egypt's frontiers, using newly acquired aircraft to bomb Egyptian airfields at El Arish and in northern Sinai. Israeli infantry captured important points in the Negev and took Beersheba, the capital of the region. Operation Ten Plagues was started and a general assault opened against the Egyptian Army which was pushed southwards. The Egyptian force inside the 'Faluja Pocket', which included amongst its officers a young intelligence captain, Gamal Abdel Nasser, was surrounded and completely cut off. The Sudanese commander, known as the 'Black Tiger', was obliged to ask permission from the Israelis to withdraw his men from the 'Pocket'. The huge Egyptian force, which had so blithely invaded Israel on the day it declared its independence, retreated in confusion back into its own territory. Several of the young officers serving with the defeated army, including Nasser and Zakaria Mohieddin, were to carry out three years later, on July 23, 1952, a well organised *coup d'état* against King Farouk and make General Mohammed Neguib, their front man, the first President of Egypt. In his book, *The Philosophy of the Revolution*, Nasser wrote that it was while he and his friends were besieged in Faluja that their decision to revolt took shape.

The second truce had now completely broken down and while the Egyptians were being swept out of the south, several Palmach units set out eastwards in the direction of Beit Jamal, in the south-western Judean Hills, in an attempt to widen the Jerusalem corridor as far as the Bethlehem-Hebron road. The force captured several Arab villages. At the same time as this force was advancing from the west, a second force was to be dispatched from Jerusalem to join the attack. At Dayan's disposal, as commander of the Israeli forces in Jerusalem, was one infantry brigade. The plan, which had been drawn up in great haste, called for an assault on the Bethlehem area and an advance upon Hebron for the purpose of capturing the Hebron hills as speedily as possible.

The rapid pace of the operation was dictated by diplomatic feelers which indicated the possibility of an agreement between King Abdullah and the State of Israel. It was apparent that the King intended to occupy the Hills of Hebron himself once the Egyptians had been ousted from that part of the country. In fact, as a pre-

79

requisite to an agreement with Israel, Abdullah wanted complete control of the Hebron-Bethlehem area, to provide an unbroken southern hinterland for Arab Jerusalem. The Israeli High Command, however, wanted to take that area before negotiations began.

The first mishap in the execution of this hastily planned operation occurred when the advance party of the attacking force delayed its zero hour. The officer commanding the party was an experienced soldier who had been with Dayan in the Lebanon in 1941. He feared his unit would be discovered in daylight and asked that the attack be postponed until the following night. Dayan accepted his argument and agreed to a postponement. Meanwhile, however, diplomatic considerations intervened. Contact with King Abdullah had been made and the order to attack was cancelled. Nineteen years were to pass before Dayan had another opportunity to return to the Hebron-Bethlehem road. This was a military defeat he was not allowed to forget for a long time.

While he was commander in Jerusalem, Dayan developed his latent talent for diplomacy. In the talks he held with Count Bernadotte, with United Nations observers and with Colonel Abdullah el Tel, Dayan demonstrated this talent by gaining strategic advantages along the cease-fire lines. His success, in improving Israeli positions along the borders with the Arab Triangle (Tulkarem-Jenin-Nablus) and in ensuring the security of the highway joining the coastal strip to the valleys inland through Wadi Ara and of the railway line from Tel Aviv to Jerusalem, aroused the ire of el Tel, who was an extreme nationalist. El Tel exploited the opportunity to fulminate against his King, whom he accused of treachery

With Shimon Peres (left) and Teddy Kollek at the Knesset in February 1955

Sinai, November 1956; Dayan with a fighting unit in the desert

Ariel (Arik) Sharon reports to Dayan following reprisal raid against Syria, 1955

Sharm el Sheikh November 1956, Dayan as Commander in Chief addresses the troops

in favouring the interests of the Jews. In the course of time, el Tel's opposition to the King became so outspoken that he was obliged to flee and seek political asylum in Cairo. There he published his memoirs in which he bitterly condemned the policy of King Abdullah. In 1951 he was sentenced to death *in absentia* for complicity in the King's assassination.

But as long as el Tel held the post of Arab Legion commander in Jerusalem, he had to obey the orders of the King. One such order, which thoroughly outraged the young nationalist officer, was to invite to Abdullah's palace two Israelis, Dayan and Eliahu Sasson, a former friend of the King. El Tel considered it a national disgrace that his country's enemies should come to the palace for peace talks. He went so far as to betray the secret of the King's intentions to young Government officials and Arab Legion officers. Yet it was el Tel himself who had helped to make the first contacts with the other side and who, in the name of the King, had opened talks with his opposite number, Moshe Dayan.

Abdullah, a son of the Hashemite Sherif Hussein of Mecca, who led the British-inspired Arab revolt against the Turks, owed his own throne to the British. He ruled over a desert kingdom inhabited by only a few hundred thousand people. To this was now added those parts of Palestine along the western bank of the River Jordan, occupied by the Arab Legion. This area included several large towns such as Nablus, Ramallah, Jenin, Bethlehem, Hebron, and the Old City of Jerusalem together with several modern suburbs to the north-east of the city. The rural population of the West Bank was relatively well educated compared with the East Bank.

F                                                         81

With Egypt, Abdullah's relations were strained, and in general, his feelings towards all the other Arab States could best be described as wary, if not suspicious. The King was a clever man and extremely realistic in his outlook. When Israel emerged victorious from the battle, he accepted the situation as it was and gave no thought to attempting a second round. He wanted to settle down and live in peace with his neighbours.

When the Egyptians had been soundly trounced in the south and the Arab armies which invaded from the north had been driven back across the borders, Abdullah thought the time was propitious for negotiations with Israel. A first round of exploratory talks was held in Paris between a representative of the King and Eliahu Sasson. Sasson, a Syrian-born Jew later to become Israel's Minister of Posts, had been the head of the Arab Department of the Jewish Agency and was on close terms with Abdullah. In fact, the King had grown fond of him, and the two men had confidence in each other.

On December 10, 1948, Dayan gave Colonel el Tel a note from Sasson for Abdullah inviting the King to open peace negotiations. Sasson suggested that he send a reliable delegate to Jerusalem to negotiate on his behalf. Two days later, on December 12, the first of several meetings took place in no man's land, near the Jaffa Gate of the Old City of Jerusalem, between Sasson on behalf of the Government of Israel, and Dr Shawkat el Setti, King Abdullah's personal physician, with whom Sasson was already acquainted. Accompanying the two delegates were Moshe Dayan and Abdullah el Tel.

But the talks held at that time were still purely preliminary and exploratory. Following a series of meetings, which continued through December, and the exchange of notes containing various suggestions, it was decided to open practical negotiations between the two countries. The Government of Israel empowered Mr Reuven Shiloah, head of the Special Assignments Department of the Foreign Ministry, to proceed with the negotiations for a peace settlement with King Abdullah. The document in which they were instructed to seek the establishment of peaceful relations between the two countries was signed by Ben-Gurion, the Prime Minister, and Moshe Sharett, the Foreign Minister.

On the other side, King Abdullah authorised el Tel to negotiate with the Israelis. El Tel, an ambitious man more concerned with his own career than with the King's wishes, created many difficulties during the negotiations. Nonetheless, he was on good personal terms with Dayan. At one of their meetings, Dayan afterwards related, he tried to persuade the Israeli officer to organise a campaign of denigration against him in the Israeli Press. He hoped that Israeli Press attacks would bolster up his image as a rabid Arab nationalist and help him to win the support of those young Arab Legion officers who opposed the moderate and pacific policy of their King. Apparently it did not occur to him that Dayan might be unable to oblige him in this respect.

Abdullah sensed el Tel's intentions of undermining the talks. In his memoirs, the Arab Legion colonel himself admits the King was suspicious of him. When he reported on the progress of the discussions, Abdullah was furious at the manner in which he was handling them. The very next day, January 11, 1949, the King telephoned el Tel and told him to bring to his palace 'the doctor's friend', meaning Sasson, and 'One-Eye', who of course was Dayan.

After dark on Janaury 16, Sasson and Dayan presented themselves at the Mandelbaum Gate in Jerusalem. Dayan was not wearing his black eye-patch and was dressed in an ordinary business suit. Abdullah el Tel was waiting for them on the other side of the Gate with an Arab Legion car and an armed escort. In great secrecy they drove rapidly eastwards. Some two hours later they arrived at the Palace of Shuna, near the Dead Sea, where King Abdullah awaited them.

Before reaching the palace, el Tel briefed them on protocol. He also told his friend Dayan of the King's idiosyncrasies. The two Israelis were received at the entrance to the palace by Dr. el Setti, who led them into a long hall in which hung a huge painting of the Battle of Trafalgar. It had been a gift to King Abdullah from King George V of England. At the far end of the hall sat the King on his throne, a short man with small but bright, intelligent eyes. To his right sat several of his Ministers, while in front sat his advisers. The visitors were seated on the King's left. The atmosphere was tense and strained, but the Monarch soon dispelled the tension with his laughter and ready wit. He presented the Israeli guests to his Court and Government and, after the short ceremony of introduction, the gathering was invited to join the King at dinner in an adjacent room. Eliahu Sasson was seated at table on the King's right-hand side, while Dayan sat on his left. Abdullah showered them with questions and in particular asked after the health of Israel's President Dr. Chaim Weizmann, the Prime Minister, and the Foreign Minister. For each of them he made a special blessing. Finally he asked after Mrs Golda Meir, who had tried to persuade him not to collaborate with the other Arab States in an attack on Israel. He made a somewhat derisive reference to Mrs Meir because she had come to see him disguised as a Bedouin woman. He had ignored her warnings at the time, and this apparently disturbed him, as he disliked the idea of having been placed in the wrong by a woman's logic. Sasson endeavoured to justify Mrs Meir's approach to the matter, but the King cut him short, saying in astonishment: 'What! I, Abdullah the son of Hussein, should accept an ultimatum from a woman?' The King seemed concerned that Mrs Meir might also participate in future talks, but Sasson set his mind at ease, informing him that she was currently Israeli Ambassador in Moscow.

Following a small helping of delicious Labaniya (a kind of yoghourt), the conversation turned to other matters. The King was a pleasant and generous host, urging all manner of Eastern dishes and sweetmeats upon his guests. His hand never left hold of a silver box containing his favourite spice which only he used.

Before getting down to the evening's serious business, the King told a number of stories, illustrating each with expressive Bedouin metaphors. He compared himself with an over-burdened horse who must get rid of part of his load if he is to reach his destination safely. Not content with speaking figuratively, he explained to his guests that, if the talks were to be proceeded with, certain disturbing factors would have to be removed so that the two countries might rapidly reach the peaceful relations they sought. He then left them, went into an adjoining room and climbed on to his bed for a nap, leaving his advisers to carry on discussions with the Israeli delegation. The King, however, left instructions that he was to be awakened the moment any difficulties were encountered, so that he could join them in the deliberations and help smooth them out.

About one hour later he returned and was informed that the talks were proceeding smoothly. When they were concluded he asked the Israelis to permit him a few days' grace for consultations with his friends, before giving his final decision. The stress he put on the word 'friends' gave the Israelis to understand that he was referring to the British and that they were backing him in the negotiations. However, when Sasson and Dayan arrived for their next meeting with him, Abdullah looked most despondent. 'They do not agree,' he said, meaning his 'friends' – the British.

British policy at that time was dominated by one motive, the maintenance of British influence in the Arab world. Hence the British viewed an Israel-Jordan entente with decided misgivings, for it might eliminate them as a factor in relationships between the two countries.

Evidence of the direction in which British pressure was exerted is provided in Dayan's own *Diary of the Sinai Campaign* (of 1956), in which he tells how, shortly before his death in 1951, King Abdullah said to him that he was ready and willing for a final settlement with Israel but that Sir Alec Kirkbride, the British Minister in Amman and Abdullah's close adviser, was opposed to the idea. Kirkbride believed that any such agreement would harm relations between Britain and Egypt.

Despite British opposition, however, the first Israeli-

Jordanian sessions at Shuna were followed by many others. During the course of the talks, Sasson was replaced by Dr Walter Eytan, Director-General of the Foreign Ministry. Others who took part in the talks on the Israeli side were Reuven Shiloah, Brigadier-General Yigal Yadin, Chief of Operations of the Israeli Defence Forces and later Chief of Staff, and Major Yehoshaphat Harkaby, who also served as a translator.

During the talks, it was suggested that a peace treaty should be based on the establishment of a confederation between the two countries, and a twelve-paragraph draft agreement on such a confederation was actually produced. It was envisaged that within the framework of the confederation the two countries would co-operate economically, and particularly in the development of natural resources. Israel would provide Jordan with an outlet to the Mediterranean, and Jordan would assure Israel of free access to the Holy Places. In the event, the draft agreement was never signed. However, the talks did succeed in ironing out a number of problems creating tension along the border.

Moshe Dayan became a frequent caller at Abdullah's palace and grew used to making the long journey from Jerusalem at dead of night. Sometimes he would set out into no man's land with Eytan, Yadin and Harkaby, at other times with Sasson or Harkaby only. Altogether, Dayan made twelve visits to the palace, and King Abdullah grew quite fond of him. He encouraged Dayan to improve his Arabic and Dayan, for his part, assured the King that, once the peoples of Israel and Jordan were at peace and on friendly terms, he would certainly polish up his knowledge of the language.

The talks continued intermittently until the summer of 1951. Dayan, by then no longer serving in Jerusalem, was one of the last Israeli representatives to see the King. By that time the King, under heavy pressure from nationalist elements, had abandoned the confederation project. Nevertheless, the nationalists, stirred up by the Mufti of Jerusalem, Haj Amin el Husseini, considered him a traitor to the Arab cause. On July 20, 1951, he was murdered as he was about to enter the Al Aqsa Mosque in Jerusalem. He was holding the hand of his beloved grandson, a boy who was to become King Hussein. With Abdullah's death, all hope of a permanent peace treaty perished.

But to return to the situation at the end of 1948, while Dayan and his colleagues were spending their first nights at Shuna, Israeli forces in the south were chasing Egyptian forces deep into the desert sands of Sinai. At the end of December Israeli troops captured the heavily fortified Egyptian positions at Abu Ageila, a performance they were to repeat in 1956 and again in 1967. The Egyptians were forced to open armistice negotiations in the Island of Rhodes, and in January, 1949, Ben-Gurion ordered all Israeli forces to withdraw across the old international frontier between Sinai and Mandatory Palestine. The armistice with Egypt was speedily concluded. In March Israel-Jordan armistice negotiations opened, also in Rhodes, under the chairmanship of Dr Ralph Bunche, the United Nations mediator.

Abdullah el Tel, who had been appointed a member of the Jordanian delegation, declined to take his place at the talks. He excused himself to his fellow officers on the delegation by explaining that it was not in Rhodes that his country's relations with Israel would be decided, but at late-night meetings at Shuna. And, indeed, there was something in what he said, for the talks held at the palace directed the delegations in Rhodes.

Moshe Dayan went to Rhodes as a member of the Israeli delegation. On March 17, in the midst of the deliberations, however, he was recalled to Israel and dispatched to Shuna for talks which were intended to prevent a crisis breaking out before agreement could be reached.

One of the points raised in Rhodes was the presence of Iraqi troops on Israel's borders with Jordan. The Government of Iraq had refused to participate in the Rhodes talks, and boasted that Iraq was the only Arab country to have waged war against Israel and never to have made peace or entered into peace discussions with her. Israel's delegation challenged the presence of the Iraqi troops and demanded the free and peaceful use of the corridor between the Israeli-held part of Samaria and the Valley of Jezreel (Esdraelon). This corridor passed through Wadi Ara where there were several Arab villages, some of which were occupied by Iraqi troops while the rest were in Israeli hands. Israel objected strongly to the Arab Legion's intention of taking over the villages held by the Iraqis when the latter withdrew. She claimed it would constitute a breach of the truce agreement signed in July the previous year. In Rhodes, the Israeli delegation refused to discuss this question with the Jordanian delegation. However, there were no objections to reaching agreement on the subject outside the framework of the Rhodes talks.

In an exchange of notes between King Abdullah and

the Director-General of Israel's Foreign Ministry, Dr Walter Eytan, the King had requested the consent of the Government of Israel to his replacing Iraqi forces, who were leaving the Arab Triangle (the Jenin-Nablus-Tulkarem area), with his own Arab Legion troops. The King referred to earlier assurances he had given Sasson and Dayan that the Iraqis would vacate the Triangle, and in fact he had just returned from Iraq where the question had been discussed with the Regent, Abdul Illah and his Prime Minister, Nuri Said. The Iraqis had agreed to hand over the sectors they held to the Jordanian forces. However, Israel was not prepared to agree to a one-sided arrangement by which the troops of one Arab country would simply replace those of another while maintaining a blockade of the road link between Israel's coastal strip and the valleys of lower Galilee.

The King was anxious to finalise this matter in order to assume control of the Arab Triangle. He, therefore, invited Dayan to the palace, and on March 19, 1949, Dayan set out for Shuna together with Major Harkaby. When they reached the palace, dinner with the King was awaiting them. Speaking in Arabic, Dayan explained Israel's interest in free and peaceful passage between the two sections of the country. He explained that, for that purpose, the Wadi Ara between Ein Shemer and Megiddo was a vitally important area for Israel. He also demonstrated that, from the strategic point of view, the strip of land was of no value to the Arabs whatsoever.

Once the King had agreed with Dayan to a solution of the problem, whereby Israel was to obtain a wide belt of land on her eastern frontier with the Arab Triangle, two Government delegations were formed to complete the

negotiations and draw up an agreement. At the head of
the Israeli delegation was Dr Eytan, while the other
members were Shiloah, Yadin, Dayan and Harkaby. An
infuriated Abdullah el Tel was later to accuse the King
of having fallen into a trap prepared for him by Dayan,
who had succeeded in depriving Jordan of Wadi Ara and
several Arab villages in the Triangle.

A few months after Wadi Ara and the villages bordering it had become Israeli territory, Devora Dayan asked
her son, Moshe, to accompany her to one of the villages
in the area. They drove there in search of an Arab house
on a hilltop. But it was not to be found. 'The house has
vanished. It's no longer there,' Mrs Dayan said sadly.
'War is war,' was Moshe's not too comforting reply.

The story behind the trip to Wadi Ara was recounted
by the ageing Mrs Dayan to her friends with that special
gift she had for both written and verbal narrative. It had
all happened many years before, when Moshe was but
nine months old. He was very ill and badly in need of
treatment. But in those days, under the Turks, the country
had few doctors. There was one who lived in Sarona, the
German Templar colony near Jaffa (today it is occupied
by the Kiria, the Tel Aviv offices of the Government).
Mrs Dayan took Moshe for the long drive by horse and
carriage from Degania to Jaffa, a distance of some ninety
miles. Passing through Wadi Ara, the child felt very sick
and cried incessantly. At the foot of a hill surmounted by
a small, blue-painted house, the carriage stopped and an
Arab who was tending his herd of goats came over to find
out what was wrong with the child. He selected a goat,
milked it on the spot, and gave the milk to the boy to
drink. Little Moshe stopped crying immediately, and the

Arab peasant went up the hill to his house and came back carrying a bottle full of goat's milk. He handed it to the young mother, promising her that her son would get well and would grow up to be a hero. Now, 35 years later, Devora Dayan wanted to show the good Arab how true his prophecy had been.

Her son had proved not only his military prowess but his flair for diplomatic negotiations, his reputation was established. During his term of service in Jerusalem, his meetings with Ministers, United Nations officials and foreign visitors, brought him into the public eye. The extremist elements in the Arab Legion considered him a dangerous enemy. To them he personified Israeli superiority both on the battlefield and at the conference table. Out of sheer angry pique, they spread a rumour that Dayan was dead and the false news was even published in some serious newspapers in Jordan. The extremist elements were even more indignant and vociferous when they learned that a joint Israel-Jordan Commission had been established in conformity with the Armistice signed in Rhodes on April 3, 1949. The object of this body was to pave the way to permanent peace. One of the two Israeli delegates on the commission was Moshe Dayan.

In addition to the Joint Commission, another body, known as the Mixed Israel-Jordan Armistice Commission, was set up. This latter was headed by a United Nations observer. It was in the Mixed Commission that Dayan put forward Israel's demands for free and peaceful passage for the railway from Tel Aviv to Jerusalem, which ran close to the Armistice lines. In order to prevent the Israelis from using the railway, the Arab Legion had occupied two villages in no man's land. The lands and buildings of these villages extended on both sides of the railway line. Dayan successfully exerted strong pressure on the Commission to have the Arab Legion force removed from the villages, in accordance with the terms of the Armistice. It had, indeed, been agreed in Rhodes that Israel should have the use of the railway. Another matter dealt with by Dayan in direct consultations with the Jordanians through the Mixed Armistice Commission was that of the division of land near the village of Beth Sefafa, south of Jerusalem. The lands of Beth Sefafa were divided in two, half being in Jordan and the other half in Israel.

Abdullah el Tel considered Dayan the major factor in forcing concessions out of Jordan, and he adopted the spurious stand that Jordan's position was sufficiently strong to have withstood the pressure put on her by Israel. In his indictment of King Abdullah, el Tel chooses to exaggerate the extent to which Dayan was able to get the better of the wily monarch. It is nonetheless true that, in his talks with the King at his palace and with el Tel in no man's land, Dayan showed himself a clever negotiator.

As early as 1949, then, Dayan showed an interest in, and a definite inclination to, direct contact with the Arabs, free of any intervention by outside forces. He believed in the efficacy of direct discussions and was the first to take the initiative and establish such contact between himself, as commander of the Israeli forces in Jerusalem, and his opposite number in the Arab Legion, without being obliged to depend upon United Nations official channels. Despite the suspicions which did exist between the two commanders, particularly on the side of el Tel, many problems in the Jerusalem sector were ironed out satisfactorily. For all that, Dayan could be and was extremely forceful when the need arose, as for example when he asserted that Israel would never agree to the internationalisation of Jerusalem and that the Jewish people would under no circumstances abandon its right to possession of the city.

The situation in the divided city was most precarious because of the close proximity of the two armies stationed within its precincts. But it might have suffered far more had it not been for the mutual understanding achieved by the two commanders. Incidents did sometimes occur, and there were casualties caused by Legionnaires sniping from the Old City walls. The Jordanian authorities refused to accept responsibility for such outbreaks, claiming on several occasions that they were individual and isolated cases. In one instance, however, they did arrest the guilty Legionnaire. Later they announced that the man had gone berserk and was to be confined to an asylum!

El Tel's nationalistic tendencies asserted themselves even in his talks with Dayan. Yet Dayan thought highly of the Jordanian officer whom he describes as being personally ambitious but well endowed with an understanding for human problems. One such problem arose over the exchange of prisoners of war. Israel held 268 Jordanians, while in Jordan there were several hundred Jewish inhabitants of the Old City of Jerusalem as well as the survivors from the Etzion Block. Dayan and el Tel reached agreement, and the prisoners were exchanged, with the exception of several dozen Jordanians who refused to leave Israel. Their intentions to this effect were transmitted in writing.

However, when it came to discussions at diplomatic

level, el Tel displayed great obstinacy and deep suspicion. On one occasion, after talks which had continued throughout the night, and after a decision had been taken granting Israel certain concessions in connection with the boundary between the two sectors of Jerusalem, el Tel stubbornly refused to sign the protocol. The American UN observer who acted as chairman of the meeting was unable to break the impasse. Dayan then took el Tel aside and quickly arranged matters with him. When they rejoined the other delegates the American officer was amazed to hear that the two commanders had reached agreement. Yet, when the time came for him to add his signature, el Tel again baulked and would not sign even though his refusal in no way affected the validity of the agreement. His national pride would not allow him to sign a document which favoured Israel. But his assurances to Dayan were not dishonoured. He pointed to a Jordanian Minister, who was a member of his country's delegation and who, at that late hour, was asleep and snoring loudly, with his head on the table surrounded by plates piled high with cigarette ends and fruit peel. 'Wake him up,' el Tel told Dayan. 'He'll sign it immediately.' Thus Dayan obtained the agreement duly signed, which enabled the Jewish sector of Jerusalem to grow and develop during the following nineteen years until it was at last reunited with the eastern sector in 1967.

# 5

## Commander-in-Chief at 38

MOSHE DAYAN MIGHT have climbed the ladder of command much more slowly had the matter been left entirely in the hands of his military superiors, most of whom had seen service with either the British Army or the Palmach. Dayan belonged to neither category. He had always been something of a lone wolf. In the opinion of the professional soldiers, namely the former British Army officers, he was too much of an individualist paying insufficient attention to basic disciplinary requirements and disdaining accepted tactics. The Palmach officers, most of whom were sheer amateurs compared to Dayan, would not accept him, because he was not their kind. Their political and social ideas, which had crystallised during the years of struggle against the British Mandatory Administration, did not appeal to Dayan. He did not view the kibbutz movement as an essential social framework for Palmach units, as they did, nor did he agree with the Left-wing political opinions which were popular among the Palmach leaders. These men, Sadeh, Allon, Galili, Carmel and the others, thought they were creating a sort of Workers' Army, along the lines of Tito's Partisans or the Red Army units during the Russian Revolution.

Fortunately for Dayan, however, Ben-Gurion also was not in sympathy with the views of the Palmach leaders.

An event which sharpened his conflict with them was the formation, in January 1948, of a new political party, to which most of the Palmach leaders declared their allegiance. This was Mapam, short for Mifleget Poalim Meuhedet (United Workers' Party), the main constituents of which were Ahdut Avoda, the Left-wing faction which had broken away from Mapai in 1944, and Hashomer Hatzair, which had begun as a Marxist-Zionist youth movement in Poland and had gone on to establish its own network of kibbutzim in Israel. The main issue which divided Mapai and Mapam in those days was that of international political orientation. Mapam was strongly pro-Soviet and in this was bitterly opposed to Ben-Gurion's own Mapai party. So great was the antagonism which developed between the two halves of the labour movement that, in the years following the birth of the State, a considerable number of kibbutzim split into Mapai and Mapam factions which established their own, separate settlements. Eventually, as the Communist bloc swung over to ever cruder anti-Zionism, Ahdut Avoda became disenchanted with Mapam's pro-Soviet line and in 1954 left the party, as it had first left Mapai.

Apart from any political motives, Ben-Gurion, as Defence Minister, foresaw dangers in the existence of an élite military corps, the Palmach, having its own separate command. In November, 1948, he ordered the Palmach Command, under Allon, to be disbanded and Palmach units to be incorporated into a unified Army. Allon, Dayan's one-time friend and colleague, interpreted this move as a personal rebuff. Another source of discontent, so far as Allon was concerned, was Ben-

G

Gurion's decision to pull back Israeli forces from Sinai at the end of 1948 when Allon had all but smashed the Egyptian Army there. Allon, indeed, was not the only officer to be dismayed at this first withdrawal from Sinai. In mid-1949, after the signing of armistices with Egypt, the Lebanon, Jordan and Syria, ex-Palmach officers began resigning from the Army. Allon was one of them.

Meanwhile, Ben-Gurion began looking around for new blood for the General Staff. What he really wanted was someone who was free both of the Palmach influence and of the rigidity of the British Army. When Dayan hove in sight, the 'Old Man' kept a close watch on him, for he knew the one-eyed warrior would fit his requirements.

By the time Allon left the Army, the General Staff had divided the country into regional commands, each headed by a brigadier-general. Allon's successor as head of the Southern Command, the biggest in area, was Brigadier-General Moshe Dayan. He was to hold the post for almost two years, until the end of 1951.

During this time the Chief of Staff (and, therefore, Commander-in-Chief) of the Israeli Defence Forces was Major-General Yigal Yadin, who had succeeded Major-General Yaakov Dori, the first Chief of Staff, who had directed the 1948 campaigns. (The highest rank conferred in the Israeli forces is, in fact, major-general, and that only on a Chief of Staff). It was Yadin who, during his tenure of office, established the organisational structure which the Israeli Army maintains until this day. Essentially, it is an Army of reservists with a small professional nucleus. Yadin, the son of the archaeologist, Professor L. Sukenik, is himself an archaeologist of international repute. When he retired from the Army, he returned to his academic pursuits. As Professor Yadin, he was to bring to the excavation of the ancient fortress of Massada the same organisational precision which, as General Yadin, he had displayed in the planning of Israel's military machine.

Moshe Dayan's new region of command, the Negev, was sparsely inhabited and there were few Jewish settlements. Yet there were enough of them to serve as targets for Arab infiltrators operating from the Gaza Strip, which was in Egyptian hands, and from the Hebron Hills, held by the Jordanians. In 1950 these raids inside Israeli territory chiefly took the form of thefts of cattle and sheep, but sometimes they ended in murder.

The military reaction to these raids was restrained. However, even then, Dayan pinpointed the need to deviate from the pattern of static defence, so as to strike at the infiltrators' bases across the frontiers. Smugglers would journey between the Gaza Strip and Jordan, taking their camels many miles across the Israeli Negev by a secret route. On the way they would rob and murder any Israeli they encountered.

Dayan instituted the system of mobile patrols in order to clear the Negev of unwelcome elements. In the course of their duties, the patrols sometimes came across Arab forces, but the ensuing incidents always remained localised. Dayan himself would often travel the length of the frontiers in an open jeep, meet the local Arab commanders and discuss with them what measures should be taken to preserve the peace. He would also see Egyptian and Jordanian soldiers guarding the borders and stop to chat freely and in a friendly spirit with them. During these trips into the Negev, Dayan became interested in archaeological sites such as Avdat and others. Out of sheer curiosity, he began to search in the sands where they looked as though they contained ancient remains. Since then he has always taken a spade along with him when travelling in the Negev.

The High Command did not ask Moshe Dayan to participate in its deliberations on strategy, except when they directly concerned his area of operations. On the other hand he did begin to be invited to discussions on diplomatic-military strategy at high Government level and was encouraged to express his opinions there.

In 1950 the United States Government made efforts to establish a military alliance of friendly States in the Middle East. This Mediterranean Alliance would have been based on Turkey and Greece, and the Americans hoped that it might be joined both by Israel and by several of the Arab States which were on friendly terms with the West.

January, 1951, found Moshe Dayan in Ankara, on what was described as a purely private visit. The Soviet News Agency Tass reported the visit as one of exploration to see whether Israel would be accepted into the projected American-backed military alliance. The Tass report was widely circulated in the Soviet Press, which accused the United States of establishing an aggressive military organisation in the Middle East centred on Turkey, Greece, and Israel. But those reports were not limited to Russia for even in the West, and particularly in America, the Press placed similar interpretations on Dayan's visit to Turkey. These comments gained substance from the fact that Ben-Gurion had visited Athens, shortly before Dayan's trip to Turkey, and had talks with

Greek Government leaders. Even a categorical denial by the Turkish Foreign Minister that there was any ulterior motive in Dayan's presence did not allay suspicion. In the end, the Mediterranean Alliance failed to materialise, but Dayan's movements nevertheless gave rise to speculation that he was a man marked out for promotion.

However, for months after his return from Turkey Dayan was hardly seen. He had nothing to do with the Mutilla operation against Syria in May, 1951, though its reverberations were felt even in his region, at the opposite end of the country. The fighting came about as a result of Syrian efforts to interfere with a large-scale Israeli project to drain the Huleh swamps, north of the Sea of Galilee. Syrian forces crossed the Jordan and seized the village of Tel el Mutilla, in the demilitarised zone on the western bank of the river. Israeli troops took up the challenge, and the position changed hands several times before the Syrians were finally expelled. But the heavy Israeli casualties caused serious concern. For the first time since the War of Independence the Army had been faced with a test of strength, and the price paid had been heavy indeed. Those responsible for the security of the State became aware that the fighting spirit of 1948 had dropped to a very low level. They realised the urgency of introducing new methods and new arms to restore Israel's military effectiveness and put some 'punch' back in her soldiers.

The Israeli Army of 1951 was largely composed of youngsters from among the new immigrants from North Africa, the Yemen and Iraq and the survivors of Hitler's death camps. These new immigrants wanted nothing but to live in peace and quiet. The law of the land required that they be conscripted for military service. But the law could not instil a fighting spirit into them, particularly as there was little fear at that time that the Arab States would launch a full-scale 'second round'. The High Command sought remedies within the framework of conventional training methods. Dayan's voice was hardly listened to. Even before Mutilla, though, he had demanded the establishment of élite units for special combat duties. The existence of such an élite, he believed, would, apart from its direct usefulness, help to raise morale in all other units. He found himself going back to the lessons of the era of Wingate, the Special Night Squads and the Palmach.

During the second half of 1951, Dayan attended a refresher course on military tactics which lasted several months and was held at a Senior Staff College in England. He returned to Israel in April, 1952 and the following month was appointed head of the Northern Command. The two years he had spent with the Southern Command had made him fully conversant with the security problems Israel faced on her borders with Egypt and Jordan. He had come to the conclusion that the focal point of Israel's security problems was, and always would be, her frontier with Egypt. The danger from Egypt became even more palpable after the military coup of July 23, 1952, which drove Farouk from his throne and gave power to Neguib, and later Nasser and his friends.

Dayan returned to the northern region on the borders with Syria and the Lebanon where, fifteen years before, he had started his military career. There he organised in the summer of 1952, the first comprehensive army manoeuvres, utilising two 'opposing' forces, ever to be held by the Israel Defence Forces. In England, he had gained much up-to-date knowledge in the deployment of large military formations, and in the green hills of Galilee two forces, the 'Blues' and the 'Greens', were put through their paces in exercises covering the whole gamut of combat, occupation and defence.

When he had completed these manoeuvres, Dayan was summoned by Ben-Gurion, and appointed Chief of Operations of the General Staff. At the same time General Mordechai Makleff was handed the baton of Chief of the General Staff by the retiring incumbent, General Yigal Yadin.

Makleff's appointment was for a limited term only. Ben-Gurion had, in fact, picked Dayan as his candidate to run the Army as early as 1950. But, although he had brought Dayan up over the heads of many other officers awaiting promotion, he could not overlook the entire list of commanders who had shown exceptional ability in the 1948 War. He, therefore, designated Makleff as Chief of Staff for the interim stage between Yadin and Dayan. During his term of office, from December 1952, until December 1953, Makleff contributed much to the organisational consolidation of the Army. Meanwhile, as Chief of Military Operations, Dayan became Number Two in the Army High Command.

The new Chief of Staff appointed a planning team to re-examine the size and strength of the Army's units, and to explore the possibilities of changing their structure. All this was to be consistent with current requirements for safeguarding the country's frontiers, and with long-range needs and developments. But it was only after Dayan's appointment as Chief of Staff, in December 1953, that these essential changes were actually introduced.

Less than one month after Makleff's appointment as Chief of Staff, Israel's paratroops carried out their first punitive action against an Arab village. The village was Falama, just inside the 'Arab Triangle', between Kalkilya and Tulkarem. Following months of infiltration from Jordan into Israeli territory for the purpose of robbery and murder, it was decided to take reprisals against one of the bases from which the saboteurs crossed the border. On the night of January 23, 1953, the action was carried out by a large force of paratroopers who set out to attack the military forces in the small village. The paratroop unit had only recently been formed. The village was under the command of the Jordan National Guard and, according to information later revealed, only 10 men, armed with rifles, were there to defend it that night. Yet they managed to repulse the Israeli attackers most successfully, despite Israeli numerical superiority.

Dayan, who had just assumed his new post on the General Staff, watched the operation that night as an observer and was amazed at the defeat of the Israeli unit. So deep an impression did it make upon him that, in every discussion he later had on the strengthening of the Israeli forces, he would remind his listeners of the miserable débâcle at Falama. The incident haunted him like a nightmare, and he began to press his colleagues on the High Command to agree to the setting up of a force with a high combat standard. Years later he was to refer to Falama as the turning point in his approach to the problem of forging Israel's military deterrent.

Dayan carried out his plan of setting up a commando

unit, which would be the envy of the rest of the Army, and which would arouse the competitive spirit of all other units. The task was entrusted to a young man named Ariel Sharon, who selected experienced and courageous fighters, among them youngsters from kibbutzim and university students, to form Battalion 101. This unit has written some glorious pages of military history in its various combat operations – in reprisal actions, in the 1956 Sinai campaign and in the Six-Day War. Several of its graduates commanded the forces which went into action in June 1967. The battalion's former chief, Brigadier-General Ariel (Arik) Sharon, commanded the southern division in Sinai during the Six-Day War.

The summer of 1953 saw no let-up in the operations of saboteurs from across the Jordanian frontier. The number of civilian infiltrators did drop considerably, but instead there were clashes with regular Jordanian troops, of both the Arab Legion and the National Guard, and these occurred all along the frontier. Israel suffered many casualties and much damage to property from Jordanian attacks on border settlements.

Many of the casualties were among new immigrants who had only recently been settled in villages specially built for them with money collected from Jews all over the world. These people, many of whom had managed to live through the Nazi holocaust in Europe, or had escaped anti-Jewish mobs in the Arab countries, now barred and bolted their windows and doors at night and lived in a constant state of fear. Not a night passed without a settlement being singled out for attack. Here the infiltrators would steal livestock; there they would walk off with irrigation pipes; elsewhere a watchman, running for help, would be murdered.

The Mixed Israel-Jordan Armistice Commission was powerless to put a stop to these Arab raids. The neutral chairman, a United Nations observer, in most cases accepted the Israeli version of the incident, and a resolution would be passed condemning Jordan as the responsible party. But the chairman would always endeavour to balance the account, so as to demonstrate his complete neutrality, by finding a pretext, based on some Jordanian complaint of a breach of the armistice agreement, to condemn Israel at the same time.

The Kibya operation was the direct outcome of these incessant attacks and the impotence of United Nations observers to keep the situation under control. The final straw was the brutal murder of an Israeli mother and her two young children by Arab infiltrators who crossed into Israel from Kibya, a Jordanian village north-east of Lydda. The Israelis decided to take reprisals.

The raid they carried out on Kibya on the night of October 14–15, 1953, demonstrated that Israeli troops were again in fighting trim. They penetrated into the village, crushed the defences and blew up almost all the houses. Those villagers who did not heed the warnings given by the Israelis that their houses were about to be dynamited, and who remained inside, were buried beneath the debris. The Kibya raid caused a furore at United Nations Headquarters, and a special emergency session of the Security Council was convened.

General Dayan served as special adviser to the Israeli delegation at that session. He was called upon to explain to the Council the circumstances which led up to the border incident. Dayan returned to Israel from the Security Council meetings in November, 1953, just before a major reshuffle took place in both the Government and the High Command.

When Ben-Gurion took a vacation during July and August, 1953, only a handful of his closest associates were aware of how exhausted the 67-year-old statesman was and of his wish to relinquish the reins of office. In September, instead of returning to his office, he declared his intention of completing a thorough survey of military and security requirements which he had started during his vacation. Experienced politicians sensed there was something in the air, but until the 'Old Man' attended the meeting of the Cabinet on October 18 there was still no indication of what he had in mind. At that time two major issues were under discussion by the Government: the repercussions of the Kibya attack, and the national irrigation scheme which required the digging of an aqueduct from the Jordan River on Israel's border with Syria. This, it was feared, could result in war with the Syrians.

As far as the Kibya incident was concerned, Ben-Gurion pointed out that he had been on leave when it happened but emphasised that, had his opinion on the matter been sought, he would have agreed to the operation. The Kibya attack had caused considerable tension within the Government, mainly between two leading Ministers: Moshe Sharett who was Foreign Minister and acting Prime Minister, and Pinhas Lavon, who was Minister without Portfolio and acting Minister of Defence. Both men were members of Ben-Gurion's party and were widely considered as rivals for the succession to the 'Old Man'.

Between Lavon and Sharett there was no love lost. Sharett was interested above all in a political solution to Israel's problems. He sought to obtain guarantees of Israel's security from the Western Powers and also tried hard to establish direct contact with Arab governments. Lavon, on the other hand, was a hard-liner. He was strongly opposed to Sharett's policy, with its emphasis on military restraint. It subsequently became known that on several occasions Lavon failed to consult Sharett before ordering operations of which the latter was likely to disapprove. Mutual recriminations filled the air, especially after the Kibya operation about which Sharett claimed he had not been properly informed beforehand.

In his book, *Things As They Are*, published in 1965, Ben-Gurion disclosed something of the Sharett-Lavon dispute. In particular, he gave the text of a number of letters sent by Sharett to Lavon. During Ben-Gurion's absence in 1953, Sharett wrote that 'it has become established procedure for the Prime Minister and Defence Minister (Ben-Gurion) to inform me beforehand of any serious retaliation to be undertaken against any neighbouring country and of any energetic measures concerning the Arab community in Israel.' This procedure, he complained, had been disregarded by Lavon. And Sharett demanded that in future he be kept fully informed.

A second letter, written a little later, was bitter and to the point: 'Your refusal to take part in consultations with your Government colleagues is most extraordinary and creates a very grave problem. If your intention is to force me to give up the task of acting Prime Minister, let me assure you that there is nothing easier. Is this indeed what you desire?'

However, at the Cabinet meeting of October 18, Ben-Gurion shelved the Sharett-Lavon dispute and concentrated on presenting his colleagues with the three-year defence programme which he had elaborated during his absence. This programme, based on the assumption that Egypt would not attack before 1956, comprised eighteen points. Among the most important were the following:

1) Strengthening of combat units at the expense of the administrative 'tail'.
2) Emphasis on striking forces (Air Force and tank divisions) and on training of commando units.
3) Creation of the technical conditions (vehicles, stores) necessary for speedy mobilisation of reservists.
4) Transfer of responsibility for supply and finance to civilian departments of the Defence Ministry, so as to leave the Armed Forces free to concentrate on purely military tasks.
5) A big educational effort to be made within the Forces to help integrate new immigrants into the nation and instil them with a sense of national pride.
6) Development of Gadna, the pre-conscription military training youth organisation.
7) Encouragement of Jewish settlement in sparsely inhabited strategic areas such as the Negev and in predominantly Arab parts of Galilee.

Only after the Cabinet had accepted this programme did Ben-Gurion make his shock announcement. He was going to resign.

Almost the last thing Ben-Gurion did before laying down his office was to appoint 38-year-old Moshe Dayan to the post of Chief of Staff of the Armed Forces, in place of General Makleff. The announcement was made on the morning of December 6, just before Ben-Gurion attended his last Cabinet meeting.

Dayan's appointment did not go unopposed. Cabinet and party colleagues of the 'Old Man' were against it. Several days earlier Ben-Gurion had received a letter from Moshe Sharett opposing the appointment. It seems that even then the veteran leaders in Ben-Gurion's party were apprehensive of Dayan's ambitions. But the 'Old Man' insisted. Just as he had brought Dayan out of anonymity in 1948, to make him commander of Jerusalem, the most sensitive area in the country from both the military and diplomatic standpoints, so he now promoted him over the heads of several officers and gave him command of the Israeli Defence Forces. Ben-Gurion did not hide his esteem for Dayan, nor his faith in his ability.

With the outgoing Army chief, General Makleff, Ben-Gurion's relations were somewhat less cordial. One of the points at issue between them concerned the transfer of certain services, such as hospitals and laundries, from military administration to civilian hands. Dayan and Shimon Peres, Director-General of the Defence Ministry, supported Ben-Gurion in demanding that the Army be relieved of responsibility for these services. On the other hand, Makleff opposed such a step, as Yadin had before him. The argument was connected, in fact, with Ben-Gurion's three-year defence plan, which itself was based on his belief that eventual armed conflict with Egypt was inevitable. He was strengthened in this belief by knowledge of the support which the Egyptians were about to receive from both East and West.

Another source of friction between Ben-Gurion and Makleff was the latter's desire to bring the civilian Defence Department, run by Peres, under the authority of the Chief of the General Staff. Makleff asked for the dismissal of Peres as well as of several senior Army officers with whom he found himself unable to work harmoniously. Ben-Gurion refused to comply with Makleff's demands, and in the end the latter retired after having served only one year in his post, the shortest time of any Israeli Chief of Staff.

It was not, indeed, to be expected that Ben-Gurion would give way and jettison Peres, whom he had singled out as one of Israel's rising stars. Peres, with whose career that of Dayan was to be intertwined, was a leading member of the younger generation in Mapai. Born in Poland in 1923, he had been a kibbutz member and a Haganah militant but had also studied at Harvard. Peres and Dayan, who both owed their promotion to Ben-Gurion, were to stand by him in a number of clashes the 'Old Man' had with his own contemporaries in the Mapai leadership.

The day after Dayan's appointment as Chief of Staff, Ben-Gurion submitted his resignation to the President. That evening he made a farewell broadcast to the nation, and the following week set out with his wife for the young kibbutz at Sde Boker which had been turned into an oasis in the desert, about thirty-five miles south of Beersheba.

Ben-Gurion announced that, after twenty years of responsibility for the security of Israel, both before and after the establishment of the State, he was mentally and physically exhausted and wanted to rest. Half his day would be spent farming and the other half reading and writing. In a message to the Armed Forces he said he was leaving them with a light heart in the knowledge that their direction was in loyal and faithful hands. He also repeated his doctrine that Israel must take care of her own destiny and not rely upon the benevolence of others.

Having selected Dayan to succeed him as the prime mover in matters of defence and security, Ben-Gurion retired to his green hut at Sde Boker. There he received important visitors, read the works of philosophers, delved deeply into Buddhist thought and worked a few hours a day in the sheep-pen. Meanwhile, Moshe Sharett became Prime Minister, and Pinhas Lavon Defence Minister, in their own right.

When he first assumed office as Chief of Staff, Dayan side-stepped controversial subjects which could have caused friction in his relations with the Minister appointed to supervise him. He concentrated more and more on building up the army into an efficient fighting machine, to be equipped with all the most modern weapons. He also carried out several organisational changes in the General Staff which, until then, had been divided into three parts: the General Staff (or operational) Branch, Quartermaster's and Manpower Branches. He added two more branches which he considered essential, and appointed two competent officers to head them. As head of the Training Branch, an area upon which Dayan laid particular emphasis, he appointed Colonel Yitzhak Rabin, and as head of the Intelligence Branch Colonel Benjamin Gibli.

Dayan concentrated his most competent officers in

these two independent branches, which previously had been departments of the General Staff Branch. He began systematically to clear the Service Corps of all officers who were potential material for combat units, whilst many of the services hitherto run by the military were handed over to civilian contractors. Of supreme importance to Dayan was the consolidation of a combat officers' corps. He lost no opportunity of emphasising that leaders and commanders counted for more on the field of battle than did plans and equipment. As he himself had always excelled at maintaining the personal touch, whether in the Army or in diplomacy, he insisted upon all officers spending time with their men. He also initiated the rule that every officer must pass a parachutist or commando course. In this he set a personal example by attending a parachute course together with senior officers of the High Command. He was almost 40 years old when he won his Parachutist Badge.

In his endeavours to transform the Army primarily into a combat force, Dayan concentrated mainly on the operational side and left his subordinates and assistants to handle matters of organisation and administration.

He cut down to the very minimum the number of officers attending military academies overseas and initiated the establishment of a Military College in Israel for officers of the rank of major and above. The training programme introduced by Dayan added a yearly complement of well-trained, competent officers and reservists to the strength of the Defence Forces. Within a few years, almost every reserve soldier and officer had undergone basic training within his unit and in combined manoeuvres. Dayan favoured and sponsored the Para-

H

chute Corps, referring to it as the élite of the army, and thus arousing the competitive spirit of commanders of other units who in consequence began to display a dynamism of their own.

As to his own military education, Dayan did not content himself with what he had studied in England. In July 1954, he went out to the United States on a tour of inspection of military installations. His visit to the Pentagon in Washington embarrassed the State Department hierarchy, who feared Arab protests and endeavoured to distort the real character of the visit. Nonetheless Dayan was received by all the top brass of the United States Army and talked with the Chief of Staff, General Matthew Ridgway. Dayan and Rabin also visited the Senior Staff Training College of the U.S. Marines. At one American military base, Dayan studied the operation of an atomic cannon. He was also permitted to take a look at the secrets of a future non-conventional war.

Dayan left the United States equipped with considerable information, but above all with new training methods which he wanted to introduce into the Israeli forces. On his way home he stopped in Paris. At that time relations between France and Israel were not yet as close as they were to become. France was only one of Israel's sources of military equipment and arms, albeit quite an important one. But, on the diplomatic level, the establishment had already begun of friendly ties of a nature which led Israel's defence chiefs to hope that France would become the major arms supplier they were seeking.

Upon his arrival in Paris, in mid-August 1954, Dayan was met by the French Chief of Staff, General Guillaume. At a special ceremony in the grounds of French Army

Headquarters, at Les Invalides, the French General conferred the decoration of 'Commander of the French Legion of Honour' upon Major-General Dayan. With the heavy chain and decoration around his neck, Dayan set out for the airport and boarded the 'plane for Israel.

When he landed at Lydda, Dayan described his visit to the United States as very useful for the Army's future. He continued to advocate constant military preparedness and said the defence problem was the major challenge to Israel during the 1950s. He called upon the youth of the country to join the select combat units which retaliated with striking efficiency against Egyptian, Jordanian or Syrian provocations along Israel's frontiers. Dayan's visit to America had given him first-hand knowledge of American combat methods using air support, and he immediately set about improving the Israeli Air Force along new and more powerful lines. In his appearances before his fellow-officers, Cabinet Ministers or Members of the Knesset (Parliament), Dayan demanded the means with which to strengthen the Defence Forces. One of his successes was the acquisition of jet fighters for the Air Force.

Dayan's maxim was 'Israel is as strong as Israel's means', and he rejected the idea that Israel must be as strong as the Arabs. He was well aware of Arab superiority in such essentials as money, manpower, territory and strategic factors. But of Israel he demanded that she make herself as powerful as material and human means permitted, through acquisition of arms, through training, military research and organisation and through a fighting spirit.

When he addressed a gathering of immigrants in one

or other of the new towns, he would turn to the young men and women and say to them: 'Israel cannot hope for outside assistance, and even if we are given weapons, they will not transform the youth of Beersheba or Ashkelon into the spearhead of our military forces. Only we, ourselves, only Israel, can do that by means of the paratroop units, the infantry, the armoured corps, the Air Force and the Army training schools.'

Dayan utterly rejected proposals to achieve a numerical balance with the Arab States. 'It just cannot be done,' was his answer. He placed the emphasis on the superior quality of the Israeli soldier. Reprisal attacks against Arab saboteurs' bases inside Jordanian, Syrian and Egyptian territory and mobile patrols along the frontiers toughened his men's fighting spirit. Yet he was not content to rely entirely upon high morale in the ranks. He organised an efficient fighting machine composed of talented young people and ruthlessly rid himself of those ageing officers bequeathed to him by his predecessors.

# 6

# The Lavon Affair

THE YEAR DAYAN became Chief of Staff was a year of serious challenges to Israel in the fields of both security and foreign policy. It was the year, 1954, in which the country celebrated the arrival of the millionth immigrant to settle there since 1948. Israel was in the throes of a dynamic development, consolidating agricultural settlements and founding new ones. The first settlement was established in the Lachish area, facing the Hebron Hills – this was the beginning of a project initiated by Ben-Gurion to populate the wastes of the northern Negev.

But it was also the year which witnessed the disruption of the solid front which had always existed in matters of defence and security. With Ben-Gurion gone from the driver's seat, the synchronisation of the political struggle with military deterrence, which had characterised his policy, was lacking. His successors, as has already been indicated, did not see eye to eye. Moshe Sharett, though Russian-born, was educated at Tel Aviv's Herzlia High School in the days of Turkish rule and served as an officer in the Ottoman Army. A graduate of the London School of Economics and a former director of the Jewish Agency's political department he had the appearance and manners of the polished diplomat and was most pedantic in his attitude towards others. Although firmly rooted in the life of the country, he lacked that self-confidence which is so characteristic of the young people not only educated but born in Israel. In adopting a policy of moderation, Sharett aimed at gaining the understanding and sympathy of world opinion, to which he was very sensitive. His reaction to the policy of military reprisals was to remark that, while mob law did exist, there was also the Rule of Law. Sharett, with his legalistic approach and his opposition to reprisal raids against Jordan, Egypt and Syria, had wielded little influence as long as Ben-Gurion was Prime Minister. In fact, Ben-Gurion would reply to Sharett's exhortations to moderation by pointing out that, when the Rule of Law became universal, its application would have meaning, but until then there was need for a defence policy which would guarantee peace.

When Ben-Gurion placed the mantle of leadership around Sharett's shoulders it was understood the 'Old Man' was quitting only temporarily. In order to ensure the continued pursuance of the policies he had established in matters of security, defence and foreign affairs, Ben-Gurion tried to install a team upon whom he could rely. Both Dayan and Peres, indeed, made no secret of their agreement with Ben-Gurion's views. The main planks in their and Ben-Gurion's platform were: the establishment of an independent deterrent force; the quest for a loyal ally who could supply Israel with the arms and military equipment she needed; the maximum utilisation of any opportunity which might arise for direct contact with the Arab States; and the establishment of a bridgehead among the emerging nations of Africa and Asia by means of technical and training assistance.

But the two young men selected by Ben-Gurion to succeed him in leading the nation were a long way from the front line of veteran politicians. Their age, their outlook, their drive and their modern approach to economic and social problems understandably aroused opposition among veteran leaders. Ben-Gurion, therefore, had to find someone in his party who in age was between the two opposing generations, who was capable of taking over the Ministry of Defence and who was acceptable to Mapai oldtimers. There was only one man who seemed to fit these requirements. Pinhas Lavon was a member of the party executive and had been Minister of Agriculture and Minister without Portfolio in Ben-Gurion's 1953 Cabinet. Born in 1904, in a small town in Galicia, south-east Poland, he was an intellectual who had for many years been classified as a 'dove'. As a young leader of the Gordonia movement, which was absorbed into Mapai, Lavon tended towards a moderate approach in relations with the Arabs. In the late thirties, when the leaders of the Jewish Agency, the labour movement and the Haganah discussed the policy to be followed regarding the Arab uprising, Lavon advocated a pacifistic line towards Arab intransigence.

In later years, however, Lavon drew nearer in outlook to Ben-Gurion. When he became a Minister he began to display definite activist tendencies and finally became an aggressive spokesman for the 'hawks'. He made good use of his rhetorical prowess and in the Knesset and elsewhere would lose no opportunity of justifying the policy of activism, as expressed in the reprisal raids.

Lavon gave Dayan a free hand when it came to retaliating against Arab provocation. Using the 101st

119

Commando Battalion, commanded by Ariel Sharon, the Army reacted rapidly and forcefully to every attack from across the frontiers. In 1954, this unit made several daring forays into Jordan. Dayan left his office at Army Headquarters to accompany the soldiers, following each stage of the operation and inhaling the smoke of battle.

Meanwhile, the security situation was causing more and more concern, not only because of the constant border harassment, but because of developments in several of the neighbouring Arab countries. In Egypt the ruling military clique had deposed General Neguib, who had attempted to restore Parliamentary government, and Colonel Nasser had installed himself as dictator.

What worried Israel was Nasser's obvious ambitions, especially in view of Western endeavours to court him. The Western Powers aimed at establishing an Eastern Mediterranean Defence Organisation. A defence pact, signed between Turkey and Pakistan in April, 1954, was intended as the forerunner of a wider agreement which would include the Arab States. That same month, the United States signed an agreement with the Baghdad Government to supply military aid to Iraq and announced its willingness to supply arms to Egypt. In July of that year, Nasser and Anthony Nutting, the British Minister of State for Foreign Affairs, signed the Anglo-Egyptian agreement whereby the British undertook to vacate the military bases they occupied in the Suez Canal Zone. These developments strengthened Nasser's hand, and he became a far more serious menace to Israel. Egyptian harassment took various forms, from shooting and shelling by Egyptian forces along the Gaza

Strip to plunder and murder by organised bands of infiltrators.

There were definite indications of frayed nerves amongst Israel's political leaders. The Anglo-Egyptian agreement on the withdrawal of British forces from the Canal Zone made no mention whatsoever of Egypt's obligation to permit the passage through the Canal of Israeli shipping. And this despite the fact that Egypt still maintained her blockade of Israel's southern sea outlet through the Gulf of Akaba and the Tiran Straits. The United Nations Security Council had been summoned to deal with Israel's complaint against this breach by Egypt of her obligations to permit the free and innocent passage of all shipping through international waters. But the Council was powerless to reach a decision, because of the Soviet veto which prevented the adoption of any resolution against Egypt.

The Israeli Prime Minister, Moshe Sharett, announced that his Government would continue its struggle against the Egyptian blockade by every legal means at its disposal. World opinion he said would be mobilised to that end. One of the means Sharett employed was to dispatch an Israeli vessel, the 500-ton *Bat Galim* through the Suez Canal. Sharett's plan was based upon his sincere belief in world opinion and in diplomatic pressure. His idea was that Egypt would be forced either to let the ship through, thereby creating a precedent, or to prove to the world that her international undertakings were meaningless.

The Government adopted Sharett's proposal, but Moshe Dayan smiled sardonically. As long as Israel was not prepared to act physically in order to ensure safe and free passage for her ships through the Suez Canal, he believed there was no point in playing with principles and precepts. He viewed the attempt to get the boat through as a worthless demonstration and dismissed the outcome in advance as a failure. He would have preferred to use force to establish command of the Tiran Straits.

The *Bat Galim* sailed from Massawa in Ethiopia towards the Suez Canal in September. On September 29, she reached Port Tewfik, at the southern end of the Canal. There the Egyptian authorities detained her and arrested her crew. The excuse given by the Egyptians for boarding the unarmed vessel was that her crew had opened fire on Egyptian fishermen in the Canal. The *Bat Galim* remained at anchor at Port Tewfik, and the Israeli crew languished in gaol until they were released three months later and returned to Israel. Sharett's demonstration made not the slightest impression upon the world at large. The Suez Canal stayed closed to Israel, as did the Tiran Straits.

It was against this background that a series of disputes erupted between Lavon and his colleagues. Friction between the Defence Minister and the Foreign Minister did not diminish now that Sharett was also head of the Government. This is proved by another of Sharett's letters to Lavon, as disclosed in Ben-Gurion's book. In May, 1954, Sharett wrote to Lavon complaining that he was not kept briefed about security affairs. 'Things are happening without my being told anything about them,' he protested. 'I hear announcements on the radio, and read them in the Press, without knowing their true background. If the correct procedure were followed, I would be told the facts, if at all possible, before the official version of them was put out. It is at all events necessary that I should be told them. It seems to me possible to have a procedure that guarantees this but the initiative for such a procedure lies with you.'

But Lavon also now came into conflict with the Dayan-Peres team. When Egypt was seen to be obtaining heavy armoured vehicles from Britain, and Iraq about to receive heavy tanks from the United States, Dayan took steps to equip the Israeli Army with suitable armour. Army experts recommended the AMX-13, a light tank made in France. Dayan examined the AMX-13 and concluded that it would be very useful as a 'tank chaser'. He, therefore, decided to order it, and the tanks were indeed to prove their worth as armoured hunters against Egyptian heavy tanks in Sinai. Peres, who had already established excellent contacts with the French aircraft industry, was instructed to go ahead and complete the deal.

This was in accordance with the understanding, which had arisen during Ben-Gurion's time as Defence Minister, that the Chief of Staff should be responsible for the choice of equipment for the Defence Forces. Lavon, however, chose to break this rule and override Dayan's decision. He cancelled the tank order. It transpired that Lavon was unable to justify his action on technical grounds. It was based on political considerations, as was shown by, among other things, a remark he made to Peres at the time – speaking of the AMX, Lavon said: 'Don't jump on the French bandwagon.' It is also known that Lavon was, in general, not in agreement with the policy of building up the Army's tank forces.

There was another way in which Dayan felt that Lavon exceeded his prerogatives. This was the Defence

Minister's holding of meetings and discussions with senior Army officers without informing the Chief of Staff. Here again Lavon was breaching an unwritten rule laid down by Ben-Gurion. Within a short time relations between Lavon and Dayan reached crisis-point.

During the first six months of the Sharett Administration, Ben-Gurion had been left in peace. In June, 1954, he entered hospital for a check-up and tests. On June 14, Dayan arrived at the hospital together with the late Colonel Argov, who had been Ben-Gurion's military aide, and Ephraim Evron, who was then Lavon's secretary. (He is now Minister at the Israeli Embassy in Washington.) Thus Ben-Gurion obtained his first intimation of the very strained relations which existed between Dayan and the Minister of Defence. Dayan gave the 'Old Man' an account of Lavon's attempts to cancel the purchase of AMX tanks and of his going behind the Chief of Staff's back to make contacts with senior staff officers. The following day Dayan wrote to Lavon tendering his resignation, but the Defence Minister pleaded with him to stay and promised to settle the misunderstandings.

Lavon was invited to call on Ben-Gurion at the hospital. Three days later the two men thrashed the matter out and Lavon assured Ben-Gurion that he would mend his fences with both Dayan and Peres. The Defence Minister backed down over the tanks dispute, and the order placed by Dayan was eventually fulfilled.

Meanwhile, news of the disharmony between the defence chiefs had leaked out. Several veteran Mapai leaders themselves called on Ben-Gurion about a month later and told him that there was a general sense of insecurity among the public. People, they said, were anxious at the lack of a strong, capable hand at the nation's helm. What worried the politicians most was the effect this might have on the forthcoming elections. Ben-Gurion calmed them down but declined their request that he return to office. Two days later yet another delegation of Mapai leaders came to see him. This group, including Levi Eshkol and Golda Meir, also complained about the open rift which had appeared between the Defence Minister and the Chief of Staff.

But whatever the dissensions which had arisen during the first half of 1954, they were as nothing compared with the storm which was about to break, and the results of which were to be felt in Israeli political life for many years to come. To understand the origins of the so-called Lavon Affair, it is necessary to turn again to the situation in the Middle East at that time. On the eve of the British withdrawal from the Suez Canal Zone, many Israelis, who had drawn comfort from the existence in the area of a foreign force which might either aid Israel or at least serve as a buffer between her and Egypt, were aghast at the thought that their country would now stand alone against Nasser. Nor were their fears diminished by the fact that the Egyptian dictator was being encouraged by both America and Russia, the two of them competing for the position of influence being vacated by Britain.

Lavon was one of those who were convinced of the gravity of the situation. He expressed a wish for direct contact with the Israeli officer in charge of military intelligence. He proceeded to develop personal relations with this officer, who laid before him a plan which, he thought, might succeed in creating conditions which would cause London and Washington to have second thoughts about their Egyptian policies. Dayan, too, was shown the plan, but he rejected it as too hazardous. In any case, Dayan did not share the trepidation of the Mapai old guard at the thought of Israel's being left face to face with the now powerful Egyptian Army. He was of the opinion that it would be advantageous to base Israel's future upon a direct confrontation with her enemies, whether in peace or war. He was also unmoved by the doubts expressed by Lavon regarding American aims in the Middle East. Dayan accepted that the United States wished to inherit British influence in Egypt but he did not believe that the American Government would be a party in any way to Nasser's aggressive designs against Israel.

These discussions took place in May and June, 1954, when it was believed that the agreement on the British withdrawal from Suez would be signed three months later. Dayan then left on his visit to the United States. While he was away, news reached Israel that the Anglo-Egyptian agreement would be concluded much earlier than originally expected. It was, in fact, signed in July. Lavon had another look at the intelligence officer's plan. During July, while Dayan was away from Israel, things began to hum. Instructions were given to go ahead with the secret operation in Egypt. It failed disastrously.*

When Dayan returned to Israel after the débâcle, he was met with a conspiracy of silence. The day following

* Publisher's note: The operation is generally understood to have been an attempt to plant bombs in the British and American Embassies in Cairo. In July, 1954, Egypt arrested eleven alleged Jewish spies; two were hanged, one committed suicide, and the others received long prison sentences. They were released, early in 1968, as part of an exchange of prisoners arranged by the United Nations Mediator, Gunnar Jarring.

his return, he went to Sde Boker to tell Ben-Gurion of the strange instructions given, he said, by the Defence Minister at a time when he, the Chief of Staff, was out of the country. He considered that Lavon's action, in going over his head, was infamous. Dayan claimed that it could have been foreseen that such an operation had not the slightest chance of succeeding. Ben-Gurion was later to emphasise that this conversation with Dayan was the first occasion on which he learned of the developments which led up to the ill-fated operation.

The Israeli military censorship attempted to suppress almost all the details of the operation, which the Press referred to euphemistically as a 'security mishap'. The general public learnt very little about it. But the Affair caused consternation among the country's political leaders. Relations between Lavon, on the one hand, and Dayan and Peres, on the other, became bitter in the extreme. The chief point at issue was not whether the order that led to the 'mishap' had been justified – in the light of subsequent events it had obviously been a mistake! – but who had given it. Lavon himself disclaimed responsibility; he said the mission had been undertaken without a directive from him. He blamed the officer concerned and pressed for his dismissal and also that of Peres. The officer, for his part, said he had acted under orders, and Lavon had given them. Sharett refused Lavon's demands, and it then became impossible for the latter to remain in the Cabinet. Early in 1955, Lavon resigned to become Secretary-General of the Histadrut, the powerful trade union federation.

Lavon's Cabinet and party colleagues had already realised that there must be changes. A delegation was dispatched to Sde Boker for the express purpose of asking Ben-Gurion to resume Government leadership. The 'Old Man' again declined. Sharett, the Prime Minister, sent personal envoys to Ben-Gurion to impress upon him the importance of his returning to the Government. One of these envoys was Golda Meir, who informed Ben-Gurion that Lavon was leaving and urged him to assume responsibility for the national defence once again.

Moshe Dayan did not participate in the drive to restore Ben-Gurion to office. He was apparently resigned to accepting Lavon's continued presence as Minister of Defence until the coming General Election. He assumed he would be able to settle the problem of his own relations with Lavon, at least temporarily. Dayan made no secret of his dissociating himself from the panicky flights to Sde Boker to get Ben-Gurion back into the Defence Ministry. He was not one of those who considered Ben-Gurion's leadership the sole solution in times of crisis. But when Ben-Gurion did return, Dayan went to receive him. He had already sensed an impending clash with the Egyptians, and expressed his satisfaction at the experienced 'Old Man's' availability at such a time.

Sharett himself had gone to Sde Boker on February 20, 1955. He entered Ben-Gurion's green-painted hut and found the 'Old Man' seated at his desk writing. The Prime Minister informed him of the Cabinet's decision to co-opt him as Minister of Defence. The next day Ben-Gurion was sworn in to his new post.

Of course, it was not only the ruling party, Mapai, which was affected by the repercussions of the Affair. The Opposition parties in the Knesset wasted no time in demanding an explanation from the Government as soon as they received the first inklings of the 'mishap'. The most aggressive line was taken by Ahdut Avoda, later to become closely aligned with Mapai under Levi Eshkol. Ahdut Avoda was the only one of the Socialist parties which could boast a few young people on its executive, and this entitled its leaders to hope they could compete against Dayan and Peres for future power. It is possible that this was one of the considerations which led the party to serve as the spearhead in the Opposition's attack on the Government over the 'mishap'. Ostensibly its barbs were aimed at Lavon, but none of the Ahdut Avoda speakers attempted to hide the fact that their real targets were Dayan and Peres. Besides the political rivalry involved, the Ahdut Avoda leaders had borne a bitter grudge against Ben-Gurion and his young aides ever since the Palmach had been disbanded in 1948.

Later on, when Ben-Gurion was once again securely seated at the helm of State, with Dayan and Peres at his side, the Ahdut Avoda leaders became the champions of Pinhas Lavon, who by then was fighting his personal battle against Ben-Gurion from the café tables of Tel Aviv.

Many thousands of words have been published about the Lavon Affair, and just as many words have been written but are still filed away and cannot be published. Several committees – of lawyers, of Army officers and of Cabinet Ministers – have delved into the secrets of the Affair in an attempt to establish responsibility for the 'mishap' of July 1954, a question which was to become the major issue in two election campaigns, those of 1961 and 1965.

The first inquiry committee, which reported in 1955,

was headed by Judge Yitzhak Olshan and included General Yaakov Dori, the 1948 Army chief. Its findings were inconclusive. In 1960 a fresh element appeared in the story when an officer detained on suspicion of espionage alleged that two other officers had induced him to give false evidence against Lavon. Ben-Gurion, as Prime Minister, set up a judicial committee, under Judge Chaim Cohn, to investigate this allegation. The committee reported in October 1960, that the detained officer, known as the 'third man', had been suborned by a Reserve officer, with the support of a Regular Army officer.*

Lavon thereupon demanded complete and public rehabilitation. He declared that he had been 'framed' by Dayan and Peres. Ben-Gurion's reply was that, if he thought he had a case, he should take it to the courts. Around this time, Sharett, no longer a member of the Government, wrote an article in which he said he was now convinced that Lavon was not to blame for the 'mishap'. There followed the establishment of a seven-member Ministerial committee, under Dr Pinhas Rosen, Minister of Justice, in an attempt to lay the ghost of the 'mishap' once for all. Alas, the haunting was now to grow even worse.

The Ministerial committee ended by exonerating Lavon. Ben-Gurion, outraged by what he took to be the whitewashing of an old colleague, thereupon resigned in February 1961, giving as his reason 'my profound concern for law and justice in the State.' Thoroughly alarmed, his party pleaded with him to return. He did so,

* Publisher's note: The 'third man' was gaoled for ten years at a secret trial. It is believed he may have betrayed the 1954 spy ring to the Egyptians.

but the price to be paid was a high one. By 159 votes to 96, the Mapai leadership adopted a proposal by Levi Eshkol to oust Lavon from his influential position at the head of the Histadrut. This marked the end of Lavon's public career. But it did not mark the end of the controversy. This flared up again in 1964. In February of that year a report appeared that Dayan had said Lavon had signed the order which led to the 'mishap'. Dayan, then Minister of Agriculture, commenting on the report at a meeting of the Knesset, explained his statement to his fellow Members of Parliament.† On this occasion Levi Eshkol, who had become Prime Minister the year before, reprimanded Dayan for going into the security aspects of the Affair in public.

Ben-Gurion, with whom the Affair hadnow become an obsession, and who had accumulated an enormous mass of evidence about it, pressed for the case against Lavon to be reopened, but the Eshkol Government, led by those who had themselves taken part in the Ministerial inquiry which exonerated Lavon, refused to do so. This did not, incidentally, save them from coming under fire from Lavon's own friends in Mapai, the so-called Min Hayesod (From the Foundations) group. Ben-Gurion's frustration in this respect was the main reason which caused him to leave the party he had led for so many years. He and his followers formed a new party, Rafi (short for Reshimat Poalei Yisrael, or Israeli Workers' List), which Dayan, too, eventually joined. The emergence of this party, with Ben-Gurion, Dayan and Peres

† Publisher's note: According to one version, Dayan had told a private gathering that Lavon signed the order four weeks after the event. Dayan indignantly denied having said this.

at its head, was the main event in Israeli politics in 1965.

Such in the briefest outline, is the history of the Affair which ruined Pinhas Lavon and demolished the political edifice constructed by the founder-leaders of Israel.

# 7

## Living from Raid to Raid

AT THE TIME of Ben-Gurion's return as Minister of
Defence in February, 1955, the Army was having a tough
job maintaining border security. Clashes along the frontier of the Gaza Strip were on the increase. These clashes
were assuming an increasingly military nature and were
obviously being organised by the Egyptian Government.
One week after Ben-Gurion's return, Israel forces attacked and invaded the Egyptian Army base at Gaza. It
was a comparatively large-scale battle in which some forty
Egyptian officers and men were killed, and about fifty
wounded. Israeli losses were ten killed, including men
from the 101st Battalion, the élite combat unit which had
seen action during the year against Arab saboteur bases
beyond the Jordan frontier.

The Israeli action did not deter the Egyptians. They
began planning a further reinforcement of their military
strength. News reached Israel in the spring of 1955 that
secret negotiations were proceeding between Egypt and
Czechoslovakia for the purchase of weapons. In April,
1955, the Egyptian High Command converted the
sabotage attacks into guerrilla warfare. They set up
Fedayeen (or Suicide) squads which operated under
direction from Egyptian Intelligence headquarters in
Gaza, and were based at three camps along the coast of
the Gaza Strip. Some 700 Fedayeen were trained by the

Egyptian Army, which later initiated the training of similar squads in Jordan, Syria and the Lebanon. Terrorist activity turned the lives of Israel's citizens into a nightmare.

Ben-Gurion's return to the Ministry of Defence had launched a decisive change in Israel's attitude towards her security problems. Both he and Dayan rejected the possibility of appealing to the Great Powers to take action to help solve these. Dayan had constantly repeated his opposition to inviting such intervention. He did not believe it would be advantageous to Israel; he feared it might tie her hands. Dayan now gained the 'Old Man's' support for his views. Dayan envisaged a preventive war against Egypt to forestall her becoming a dangerous threat to Israel's existence. In one of their talks, in which Dayan revealed the lines along which he was thinking, Ben-Gurion asked: 'So you want a war?' Dayan gave his usual smile and replied: 'No. No, I'm not in favour of our beginning a war, but I shall object to concessions of any sort, and if the Arabs ask for war, they shall have it. If the Syrians open fire on us when we try to divert the Jordan waters, our reply will be war.'

By stepping up their policy of aggression, it was the Egyptians who virtually dictated Israel's actions. Concurrent with the ban imposed upon the passage of Israeli shipping and cargoes through the Suez Canal, Egypt tightened the noose on the Tiran Straits. Not satisfied with preventing Israeli ships from using the Straits, she now extended the blockade to the air space above it. All international air and shipping lines were informed that the Tiran Straits were within Egyptian territory, and henceforward permission to pass through or over them must be applied for from the Egyptian authorities seventy-two hours in advance. It was made eminently clear that permission would be denied to Israeli shipping, aircraft, cargoes or passengers. Because of these instructions, which were issued in September 1955, El Al, the Israeli national airline, had to cancel its regular flights from Tel Aviv to South Africa over the Red Sea.

The Egyptian blockade of Israel's southern port of Eilat was the final blow which convinced the country's leaders of the necessity of using force against Nasser. It had become obvious there was no possibility of reaching peaceful understanding with him.

The American Government was persisting in its efforts to gain the Egyptian President's sympathy. Negotiations were under way for the United States to finance, at a cost of hundreds of millions of dollars, the construction of a hydro-electric dam at Aswan, on the Nile. At the same time, Nasser's delegates were discussing the purchase of huge consignments of arms in Moscow and Prague. And all this despite the fact that, from the economic viewpoint, Egypt was on the verge of bankruptcy! To finance the huge arms deal with the Soviet bloc, Nasser had been obliged to mortgage his entire year's cotton crop. Yet he continued to play off each side against the other. In Cairo he held talks with John Foster Dulles, the American Secretary of State, and in Moscow he saw Khrushchev.

The defence team set up by Ben-Gurion in the latter part of 1953 began developing new and enterprising lines of action. Shimon Peres, on one of his European trips that year in search of arms, had made the acquaintance of Marcel Dassault, the head of one of the large French aircraft manufacturing concerns. During their conversation he touched on the question of whether it would be possible for him to meet the French Deputy Prime Minister, Paul Reynaud. The French Jewish industrialist, who was particularly interested in forging friendly relations with his Israeli client, made good use of his connections in high places, and a meeting between Peres and Reynaud was arranged. When Peres (then only 30 years old) left after his talk with the French Deputy Prime Minister, he had a feeling that the chances of France's fulfilling Israel's arms needs were bright indeed.

The French Government was constantly changing in those days, and Peres was careful to maintain the closest possible contact with all the military chiefs and political party leaders who followed one another in and out of office. He became a constant and welcome visitor in both military and political circles in Paris. Right-wingers and Left-wingers alike held doors open for him. They saw in Israel and the Israeli Army a possible future ally at a time when the Fourth Republic, after giving in to Tunisian and Moroccan nationalists, was becoming bogged down in a bloody war against the Algerian revolt, which broke out in 1954.

Peres had a flair for making friends and did so to good effect among the very highest echelons of French generals. During Pierre Mendès-France's tenure of office as Prime Minister, Peres became closely acquainted with General Pierre Koenig, then Minister of Defence. When Edgar Faure became Prime Minister, Peres gained the friendship of his Defence Minister, General Pierre Billotte. Similarly, when Guy Mollet became Prime Minister, Peres made friends with both the Foreign Minister, Christian Pineau, and the Defence Minister, Maurice Bourgès-Manoury.

In the summer of 1955 Peres was in Paris. He had a meeting one morning with Bourgès-Manoury, who was then Minister of the Interior and responsible for Algerian affairs. Also present was Abel Thomas, Director of the Department. It was agreed at that meeting that France would supply arms to Israel, even beyond the limits of ordinary commercial contracts with French armament and aircraft manufacturers. Peres' French friends suggested that he should maintain direct contact with the French Army, and not via normal diplomatic channels. Moshe Sharett, who was then both Prime Minister and Foreign Minister, objected strongly to such an arrangement, but Ben-Gurion, the Minister of Defence, tipped the scales in favour of Peres' opinion that it would be of advantage to Israel to accept the French suggestion. This disagreement between Ben-Gurion and Sharett worsened the already strained relations between the two statesmen; they had for some time been at variance because of their different attitudes on matters of foreign and defence policies. This split among veteran Mapai leaders over the behaviour of the 'Young Turks', Dayan and Peres, was perpetuated when Golda Meir succeeded Sharett as Foreign Minister in 1956. She, too, complained bitterly at Peres making his own diplomatic contacts without going through the Foreign Ministry. However, Peres' contacts in France opened up new horizons for Israel, even beyond his own field of arms procurement.

Dayan, who was well known to the French High Command since his investiture by General Augustin Guillaume as a Commander of the Legion of Honour, was given the task of fostering military liaison with the French. He, too, found a ready welcome awaiting him in

France. He made personal friends of several French generals on active service, for they recognised in him a fine military leader, although they did not spare him their badinage over his missing eye which, they would remind him, was lost when fighting with the British against the French; true, it was against the Vichy French, who were collaborating with Nazi Germany!

During one of his visits to France, in October 1955, when he was combining a vacation with visits to military establishments and arms and aircraft factories, Dayan received a cable from Tel Aviv in which Ben-Gurion requested him to return to Israel immediately. He returned home and went to see Ben-Gurion the next day at his hotel room, where the 'Old Man' was confined to bed, and gave him an up-to-date review of the security position in the country. When Ben-Gurion had heard the report, he ordered Dayan to make preparations for the military occupation of the Straits of Tiran, namely the two islands, Tiran and Sanafir, which commanded the entrance to the Straits, and Sharm-el-Sheikh and Ras Nasrani, on the southern coast of the Sinai Peninsula, where Egyptian artillery batteries were located.

The following week, early in November 1955, after the elections to the Third Knesset, Ben-Gurion again became Prime Minister as well as keeping Defence. In his speech to the House, in which he introduced the new Cabinet, Ben-Gurion stated that Egypt was blockading Israel's outlet to the Red Sea in direct contravention of international maritime law. 'This unilateral warfare must stop,' Ben-Gurion declared, 'or it will not remain unilateral for long. We are ready to make peace, but not to commit suicide.'

A discussion was held in the Cabinet following the Prime Minister's speech in the Knesset and it was resolved that the time was not propitious for a military operation to open the sea lanes to Eilat, but that Israel considered herself free to act wherever and whenever it was found to be most advantageous.

The Government's decision prompted Dayan to write a letter to Ben-Gurion saying Israel's failure to take immediate military action to ensure free access to Eilat would be interpreted as acceptance of the restrictions imposed by Egypt. He asked for authorisation to carry out the occupation of the Tiran Straits within one month and warned that any delay would tend to reduce Israel's chances of achieving a military success. Dayan began to press for the purchase of more jet fighters capable of coping with the Soviet MiG-15s which Egypt was beginning to receive following her arms deal with Czechoslovakia.

Dayan also warned against placing much reliance upon the United Nations and its representatives in the area. He considered the UN Truce Supervision Organisation as nothing else than a 'complaint box' in which each side deposited its complaints against the other, while the UN observers were helpless to prevent the deterioration of conditions along the borders. The fact that the then UN Secretary-General, Dag Hammarsjöld, and the Chief UN Observer, the Canadian General Burns, were unable to extract a promise from Nasser to stop Fedayeen operations in Israel was viewed by Dayan as yet further proof of the international organisation's impotence.

There was tension along Israel's other frontiers, too. Infiltrators continued to slip across from Jordan on errands of robbery and murder, while in the north the

Syrians used their artillery emplacements on the Golan Heights to shell Jewish settlements in the Huleh Valley. They would also fire at Israeli fishermen on the Sea of Galilee. During the fishing season Israeli boats were at the mercy of the Syrians, who had established positions along the eastern bank of the lake – in defiance of the armistice agreement and the international demarcation lines, according to which a swathe of land several yards wide along the entire eastern bank was Israeli territory.

Israel decided to retaliate against this aggression despite the strong topographical advantage possessed by the Syrians, whose positions were solidly entrenched along the mountain tops. An Israeli commando battalion launched a night assault. Several Syrian strongpoints and bunkers were destroyed and over 30 Syrian officers and men, belonging to the units which had been shooting at Israeli settlements and fishermen, were taken prisoners.

But by the spring of 1956, the centre of concern had again moved southwards. Tension had risen on Israel's southern and eastern frontiers, particularly along that of the Gaza Strip. Since the beginning of the year, not a day had passed without an attack by Fedayeen squads which crossed over from the Strip. Invariably the marauders' tracks led back across the Gaza border towards the bases established by the Fedayeen. There were indications that the guerrilla bands in the Strip were co-operating with terrorists based in Jordan. One of the most horrible murders was perpetrated by Fedayeen who managed to penetrate into Kfar Habad, an Orthodox religious village some eight miles east of Tel Aviv, and attacked a synagogue filled with children. While they were at prayer, the Fedayeen opened fire through the windows, slaughtering a teacher and five boys and wounding several others. The tracks of the murderers, who had come from the south, led eastwards in the direction of Latrun, in Jordanian territory.

That same night the murderers struck again. This time they attacked a vehicle of the Israeli Border Patrol force driving near Lydda. One Israeli soldier was injured.

The murder of the children at Kfar Habad horrified Israelis and aroused deep feelings of anger. Once again the Government was obliged to give the green light to a reprisal raid. This time something more convincing was needed.

Two days after the Kfar Habad massacre Dag Hammarsjöld arrived in Israel for talks on a previous Israeli complaint which contained details of some 200 cases of murder and sabotage perpetrated by Egyptian terrorists during the past four months. Hammarsjöld went on to Cairo and from there announced that Nasser had undertaken to put a stop to such incidents. April 18 was given as the date upon which all hostile acts were to cease. The UN Secretary-General believed he had achieved a cease-fire agreement, but hardly had he left Egypt when, on April 29, the Fedayeen carried out yet another murderous attack.

The victim this time was a young Tel Avivian, Roy Rothberg, who had left the home of his well-to-do parents in town and joined a group of young men and women who, after completing their military service, established a kibbutz in the sandy dunes opposite the Gaza Strip. Two days earlier Dayan had visited the new kibbutz, named Nahal Oz, and had been impressed by young Roy who was its secretary and one of the leaders of the group.

141

On the morning of the murder, Roy was walking across the newly ploughed fields of the settlement when he was killed by Egyptian bullets. Dayan returned to Nahal Oz to attend Roy's funeral. It proved to be one of the rare occasions when he was visibly moved. His single eye was seen blinking back a tear. He walked slowly towards the freshly dug grave of the young victim and, in a moving eulogy, declared: 'Roy's blood cries out to us and accuses us only, for a thousand times have we sworn that our blood shall not be spilled in vain, and yet we allowed ourselves only yesterday to be cajoled into listening and believing. And meanwhile Roy was murdered from ambush,' Dayan was referring to the promise of peace which Hammarsjöld thought he had obtained in Cairo. Dayan completed his eulogy by saying: 'It is the fate of our generation that our life requires that we be always prepared and armed, strong and determined, for if the sword be struck from our grasp, we shall die.' Dayan's words at Nahal Oz sadly summed up the impasse in which Israel found herself.

The reprisal raids had been initiated by Dayan in an attempt to set a high price on Arab acts of murder and destruction. But by now he was beginning to have doubts as to their efficacy. There were many obvious drawbacks to these nocturnal forays into Arab territory. Israeli losses were heavy, although the Jordanians and Egyptians suffered far heavier losses. Furthermore, the 'hit and run' system used in these massive reprisal operations did not seem to be having the same effect as it had when first introduced. Then, indeed, it had appeared to create a strong impression on the Arabs and deter their Governments from challenging the Israeli Army.

It was after the murders of the children in the synagogue at Kfar Habad and of Roy Rothberg in the fields of Nahal Oz, that Dayan made up his mind to use other methods. He had in mind the capture of an objective across the border, an objective he could hold on to as a bargaining counter which could be exchanged for Arab guarantees of security, at least for the area immediately involved. But Dayan could obtain no backing in the Government for his plans. Ministers feared to take any action which could be interpreted as territorial conquest. Even when a unit of Jordan's Regular Army participated in an act of aggression against Israel, the Government would not relax its decision.

The Government met once again to discuss whether action should be taken against Jordan following a serious incident in Jerusalem on September 22, 1956. Arab Legion soldiers entrenched in the Mar Elias Monastery on the road to Bethlehem, opened heavy fire on a group of civilians taking part in an archaeological conference who were visiting an ancient site at Ramat Rahel on the southern outskirts of the city. Four archaeologists were killed in that attack and 16 wounded. The Legionnaires had poured machine-gun fire into people armed with nothing more lethal than guide books and diagrams of the Ramat Rahel archaeological excavations. The next day another attack was carried out by Arab Legion troops on unarmed civilians. This time the victims were a woman and her daughter from the village of Aminadav who were out in the fields collecting firewood. Shots were fired at them by Legionnaires stationed in the Arab village of B'tir, and both women were killed instantly.

It was clear to Israel that these acts of wanton murder

by the Arab Legion were not isolated incidents but links in a chain of aggression initiated by Egypt and Jordan. Dayan requested authority to carry out a reprisal action on such a scale as would serve to deter whatever elements were responsible for these acts of aggression. His intention was to make the type of massive commando raid on a Jordanian objective as he had on Khan Yunis, in the Gaza Strip, and Kuntilla, about fifty miles north of Eilat, in August and October 1955, in retaliation for Egyptian aggression. On September 25, following the attacks at Ramat Rahel and Aminadav, he went to see Ben-Gurion and suggested four possible Jordanian objectives. In his diary, Dayan writes that he selected military objectives only in order to avoid involving civilians. Ben-Gurion, however, was content with a limited reprisal raid in the Jerusalem Hills.

That night an Israeli commando unit attacked the police station at Hussan. Dayan, as usual, went out with the attacking force, remaining with the forward command post. He was still the combat officer who joins his forces on the battlefield and sets an example by giving the command 'Follow me!' instead of 'Forward!', even though he had been Chief of Staff for the past three years. Dayan admits in his diary that he preferred to watch an operation at close quarters and, when necessary, even to intervene in its management, although he could well imagine that the officer in command might not be overjoyed at having the Chief of Staff peering over his shoulder. Dayan paid no attention to the exhortations of his staff not to take such tremendous risks. He had, indeed, several very close shaves. During the Hussan operation, a Jordanian shell exploded close to the forward post in which he was lying. Nothing happened to him, but when he returned to Kibbutz Mevuot Betar, in the Jerusalem Hills, he found that his driver had been wounded, together with several other men who had stayed behind in the rear command post. When he saw Dayan, the injured driver apologised to him for not having taken his advice and stayed out in the open during the Jordanian shelling. Dayan told him: 'During action be out in an open field and not hidden behind cover. Your lucky star up in the heavens can't see you behind a fortified position and won't be able to take care of you.'

But few lucky stars seemed to have had much effect during that operation. The Hussan police station was destroyed and the Arab Legion left forty dead and dozens wounded on the field of battle. But the Israeli force paid dearly for it. Ten men were killed and sixteen wounded. The courage of the men of the commando force has become legendary amongst Israel's younger generation. One of the heroes of the Hussan battle was Captain Meir Har-Zion, a villager and a student who had volunteered for service with the 101st Battalion. He never missed an operation, even when he was not called upon to participate in it. In Hussan, a Jordanian bullet struck him in the neck and the 21-year-old Har-Zion fell to the ground unable to breathe. The medical officer rushed to him and with a penknife made an opening in his windpipe, which was clogged with congealing blood. Har-Zion survived and, like all the officers of his unit who suffered injuries in such operations, went on to fight in the 1956 Sinai campaign and in the 1967 Six-Day War.

After returning from the Hussan operation, Dayan drew up a balance sheet showing the pros and cons of

K                                                                    145 reprisal raids in general and came to the conclusion that the value of the system had been exhausted. The restrictions imposed upon the attacking force were legion. It had to operate at night, overcome enemy resistance, meet whatever reinforcements might arrive, carry out its mission, which was usually the dynamiting of a military objective, and then return to base, still at night, without leaving any of the dead or wounded behind. These restrictions greatly limited the chances of success, particularly when the number of such actions carried out ruled out the important element of surprise. But a fortnight later, before a final decision could be taken regarding the cessation of the night reprisal method, the Army was to carry out one of the biggest raids of this kind.

The reprisal action at Hussan did not deter the Jordanians, and they continued their murderous assaults. Their next objective was in the central sector of the country, the narrow coastal strip between Natanya and Tel Aviv. In broad daylight a group of Jordanian saboteurs penetrated into Israel and, from ambush, killed two Jewish labourers working in an orange grove near Tel Mond. The murder of the two men caused a furore in the Israeli High Command. The fact that Jordanian saboteurs were able to walk abroad in full daylight in the very heart of the country convinced the Israelis that prompt action must be taken. It was obvious that the Jordanian terrorists were receiving the backing and encouragement of King Hussein. Israel had notified him of the names of Jordanian soldiers identified as having committed murders inside Israeli territory. He had been asked to arrest the men and mete out suitable punishment. In the event, although the men were arrested, they were released upon the express instructions of the King, before even being brought to trial.

Dayan selected the police station at Kalkilya, directly opposite the Israeli township of Kfar Saba, in the Sharon coastal strip, as his target for a massive reprisal action. This time it was his intention to make a lasting impression upon the civilian residents of the West Bank, for it was they who were providing aid and comfort for the murderers. Some 20,000 people lived in Kalkilya, and it was thought that the blowing up of the fortress-like police station should indeed have a deterrent effect upon the population.

When Dayan presented his plan of action to Ben-Gurion on October 10, the 'Old Man' specifically asked that he avoid extending his attack into the town itself, so as to spare the lives of civilians. On that condition, Ben-Gurion approved the plan and presented it to the Government for final confirmation. While the Government was in session discussing it, Dayan summoned the paratroop commander and gave him his battle orders. The attackers were to have artillery support, and the target would be brightly illuminated by giant searchlights capable of lighting the area from a distance of almost two miles.

The members of the High Command were not happy at the pace set by Dayan in organising this attack. They were concerned lest the haste with which the preparations were being made resulted only in heavier casualties to the attacking force. But Dayan was insistent and hinted to his officers that there were diplomatic considerations to be taken into account.

147

The officers did not then know that within two weeks they were to be at war with Egypt.

The Jordanians were ready for the Israeli attack on Kalkilya. The commando force was met with powerful answering fire. The Israelis were accustomed to attacking without artillery support and called off the shelling sooner than was really necessary. The softening-up barrage by Israeli field guns, if continued, might have made the final storming of the police fortress easier. The Israelis took their objective in fierce hand-to-hand fighting, and the building was blown up. But the cost was high. The heaviest casualties were suffered by the unit sent to keep reinforcements from eastern Kalkilya coming to the rescue. The Jordanian Army managed to get some men through the Israeli lines, and they set up an ambush westwards of this covering unit. In the fierce battle which ensued, the Israeli force suffered heavily. In order to liberate the trapped unit, armoured vehicles were dispatched to the scene, and four Israeli aircraft flew over the battleground. However, strict orders were received not to capture any positions across the frontiers. Israeli losses in this action were eighteen men killed, including eight officers, and more than fifty wounded. These men belonged to the finest combat unit in the Army, and it was they who had borne the brunt of the many reprisal raids carried out inside Arab territory.

World reaction to the Kalkilya operation was very serious. Britain had threatened to use the Royal Air Force against the Israeli attackers at Kalkilya, and this marked the first time such a threat had been uttered. The British Chargé d'Affaires even informed Ben-Gurion that a division of Iraqi troops was ready to march into Jordan as reinforcements and that, if Israel carried out further military operations against Jordan, Britain would go to Jordan's aid. Britain had a defence pact with Jordan, and King Hussein was demanding its implementation. The British, for their part, were concerned to bolster up King Hussein's position, as they wished to prove to him that Britain was still a strong arm worth leaning upon, even though he had summarily dismissed the British Commander of his Arab Legion, Glubb Pasha.

The British wished to strengthen their ties both with Jordan and with Iraq, in which latter country Nuri Said, a great friend of Britain's, was Prime Minister. He was to be murdered less than two years later when General Kassem deposed the Monarchy and assumed power. Nuri Said had suggested that the Israel-Arab dispute could be settled by going back to the United Nations Partition Plan of November, 1947, with the proviso that the Arabs be given Galilee and the Negev. In London there was support for Nuri Said's suggestion. In Israel the British threat of force was seen as an indication of British willingness to compel Israel to accept the Iraqi Prime Minister's plan. The proposed entry of the Iraqi Army into Jordan was interpreted by Israel as a first joint step by Jordan and Iraq, with British connivance, towards carrying out the Iraqi scheme. Israel issued a warning that she reserved the right to act if the status quo on her frontiers were altered by the appearance of Iraqi forces in Jordan.

Britain at that time was in the most anomalous of situations. On the one hand she stood behind Jordan and Iraq against Israel, while on the other she was secretly preparing to launch an operation, in which Israel was to play a vital part, to capture the Suez Canal, which Nasser had nationalised. At all events, while British fulminations over the Kalkilya attack drew the world's attention to the Jordanian front, Israel was enabled to go quietly ahead with her preparations on the southern front in anticipation of the Sinai campaign, due at the end of the month.

The background against which the invasion of Sinai had been decided on was one of deepening Arab hostility, aggravated by the support given to the Arabs by the Great Powers. Israeli overtures to join NATO or to conclude a diplomatic or military alliance which would guarantee the young State's security had come to nothing. Dayan, with his reprisal raids, had made the Arabs pay a heavy price for their aggressiveness. But in the political sphere the raids caused great trouble. Israeli statesmen feared the complications their continuance could cause with friendly countries, particularly the United States. Dayan had claimed that there was no alternative to the raids but finally he made up his mind to implement a different system.

After Kalkilya he called a conference of Israeli newspaper editors and tried to get them to follow his thoughts on the steps Israel should take. He warned that the consequences of not reacting to Arab provocations would be to make life in Israel impossible. Yet limited reprisals had failed to stop the constant infiltrations by murderers and saboteurs. The next step in the logic of deterrence was the capture and occupation of one of the bases from which the infiltrators operated and its retention as a bargaining counter. And when it came to the question of conquest and occupation, there was no point in going for a small objective.

It is not known when exactly Dayan began thinking in terms of the Sinai campaign, of which he was the prime mover. But in March 1956, he had warned of a war which would break out before the year was over if the Egyptians continued to harass Israel with sabotage raids and maintained their sea and air blockade. The orders he had received the previous year from Ben-Gurion to plan the capture of the Tiran Straits were still fresh in his mind, even though opposition within the Government had prevented execution of the plan. If he had any doubts now about the advisability of war, the establishment on October 24 of the Joint Arab Command, combining the forces of Egypt, Jordan and Syria, probably ended them.

# 8
## Victory in Sinai

DAYAN WAS CONFIDENT in the ability of the Israeli
Defence Forces to deal a knock-out blow to the Egyptian
Army in Sinai and to break the blockade of Eilat. He
managed to infuse his Staff officers and members of the
Government with his own confidence, and Ben-Gurion
was content to rely upon his judgment. The 'Old Man'
was, however, concerned at the price Israel might have
to pay in civilian lives in the event of open warfare with
an Egypt equipped with Soviet jet fighters and bombers.
Furthermore, Ben-Gurion was still hoping for a suitable
political opportunity to arise which would make it easier
for Israel to embark upon a preventive military operation.

While Dayan busied himself with his plans and got his
forces into fighting shape, Shimon Peres, the junior
partner in Ben-Gurion's triumvirate, was strengthening
his ties with French statesmen, military leaders and arms
manufacturers. In 1956, Israel's arms purchases in
France were shifted on to a far broader base. The rise in
Israeli requirements for jet aircraft and tanks aroused
considerable interest in French military circles. The
French generals began to look upon Israel as a potential
military power in the Middle East. Franco-Israel relations
began to take on an entirely different aspect with the
advent of the Israeli Army at the conference table of the
French High Command.

The French, who were then fighting in Algeria, considered Nasser the driving force behind the revolt of the F.L.N. Several of the leaders of the French Socialist Party, such as the Prime Minister, Guy Mollet, or the Foreign Minister, Christian Pineau, may have been influenced by feelings of sympathy for the justice of Israel's point of view, but what actually decided the issue in Israel's favour were the hard-headed straightforward military considerations of the French Army, which wished to see Nasser's influence diminish. Israel thus became a virtual ally of the French in their plans to counter Nasser's intervention in Algeria and his seizure of the Suez Canal.

In place of supplies from surplus military stocks, Israel began to receive the latest equipment produced by French manufacturers. This was made possible by the recommendation of the French High Command, and deliveries were often made from the latter's own stocks. Relations between France and Israel became in a very short time extremely close. But this friendship was kept distinct from the official relations between the two countries as conducted by their Foreign Ministries. The Quai d'Orsay maintained its traditional policy of neutrality in the dispute between Israel and the Arab States and even stood by the US-French-British agreement of 1950 to limit the flow of arms to the area. It was Foreign Minister Pineau personally who established the pro-Israel policy, with the agreement of both the Prime Minister and the Defence Minister, Maurice Bourgès-Manoury.

Dayan was still waiting for the order from Ben-Gurion to use military force to open the sea-way to Eilat when, on July 26, 1956, Nasser announced the nationalisation of the Suez Canal. This was a serious blow to Britain, France and the other maritime nations which were the major shareholders in the Canal. They greatly feared that Nasser's move would mean an end to freedom of passage through this international waterway. The next day, Britain's Prime Minister, Sir Anthony Eden, informed General Dwight Eisenhower, the United States President, that Britain was considering the use of force against Nasser. It was on that day, too, that Shimon Peres arrived in Paris from London. Joseph Nahmias, his agent in the French capital, who played a leading role in establishing the relations between the French and Israeli security forces, had arranged a meeting with Bourgès-Manoury at the latter's home. The subject discussed was the new situation caused by the nationalisation of the Canal, and Peres, noting the obvious signs of vexation on his host's face, broached the idea of a joint action to break the blockade of the Gulf of Akaba and to ensure freedom of passage through the Suez Canal. The idea made sense to Bourgès-Manoury. Although at that time Peres had no authority to make such a hazardous suggestion, his brainwave elicited a favourable response both in Paris and in Jerusalem. What it boiled down to was that the French would supply military aid, including munitions and equipment, to Israel to enable her to occupy Sharm-el-Sheikh and to rout the Egyptian Army threatening her borders.

Secret discussions in Paris and Israel followed the meeting between Peres and Bourgès-Manoury. The talks were soon joined by the two Foreign Ministers, Pineau and Mrs Golda Meir, who had by now taken Sharett's place in the Israeli Government. By the end of the summer, General Dayan came into the picture after several of his Staff officers had already held discussions with their colleagues of the French High Command.

While talks were proceeding in Paris regarding the arms supply, Israel learnt of the Franco-British plan to occupy the Canal Zone. A telegram from Israeli military representatives in Paris reported that the Anglo-French Operation Musketeer was due to be launched in a matter of weeks and would be commanded by the British General Sir Charles Keightly and the French Admiral Barjot. Dayan realised that his opportunity had come and placed the Defence Forces on the alert.

In his *Sinai Diary*, Dayan tells how the telegram from Paris arrived on September 1, during a conference of the Israeli General Staff, attended by Ben-Gurion, to discuss armoured force strategy. It was immediately decided to place the Army on a war footing. In the days following, Dayan visited Air Force and armoured units and gave orders to speed up the training of the crews to man the new tanks Israel was receiving and to prepare the new French planes for action. The General Staff was instructed to examine a number of operational plans, ranging from full conquest of the Sinai Peninsula to occupation of the Straits of Tiran or the Gaza Strip only. Dayan then accompanied Shimon Peres to Paris, travelling via Tunis, in order to complete negotiations regarding the supply of French arms. On October 1, the two men arrived at the private home of the political adviser to the French Minister of Defence where, in great secrecy, they met with the top brass of the French Army, headed by the French Chief of Staff, General Ely.

The French officers had come back from holding talks

with their British colleagues in preparation for Operation Musketeer. They were unhappy when they returned from London. They could find no way to overcome the atmosphere of indecision and doubt which had characterised the talks on the British side. There had been times when the French were on the verge of backing out of the joint venture just because of the scepticism their British allies displayed regarding the chances of success. It went without saying that there could be no doubt as to the outcome of the military side of the operation, yet the British still managed to find fault with it.

One of the French officers involved, General Challe, then Deputy Air Force Chief of Staff, told an Israeli diplomat at the time that the French were in despair at the British attitude. Later, after Dayan's arrival, Challe told the same diplomat that it was the Israeli Army chief who had inspired them with fresh hope. 'In contrast to the sluggishness and lack of confidence shown by the British', declared Challe, 'Dayan's clear and dynamic attitude was most striking. He knew exactly what he wanted and what it was in his power to achieve.'

The French drew courage from Dayan's self-confidence, yet he frightened them with his daring approach and his conviction as to his Army's chances of defeating the Egyptians. He did not then take into account the direct assistance of any other armed force. The French drew his attention to the British doubts, to which Dayan replied that the Israelis knew the Egyptian strength better than did the British.

General Ely asked Dayan how long he estimated it would take the Israelis to reach the Suez Canal. That, Dayan answered, depended entirely upon the speed of the vehicles at their disposal. Loud laughter rang through the elegant salon in which the meeting between the French and Israelis was being held. General Ely, a tall, lean, professional soldier, who treated the military operation under discussion with great seriousness, feared there might be an undercurrent of recklessness in Dayan's attitude. Nonetheless the Israeli General made a great impression upon him because of his unwavering self-confidence and the clarity with which he analysed the facts and evaluated the situation.

Dayan presented the list of equipment he needed. This included tanks, tank-carriers, armoured vehicles, aircraft and other items. When General Ely heard what the composition of the Israeli units was, and the enormous task they were taking upon themselves, his eyebrows shot up and a look of sheer astonishment came into his eyes. But Dayan and Peres left the meeting with a written assurance that they would have the equipment needed with which to begin the campaign. That evening, just before boarding the French military aeroplane which was to take them back to Tel Aviv, the two conspirators took a short stroll through the streets of Paris. Dayan wore dark sunglasses as a disguise. But they did not prevent his being recognised by a number of Israelis who came across him on the Champs Elysées. 'Wow!' one exclaimed, at the sight of him and Peres. 'Something must be going on here if those two are walking about incognito.' Less than a month later they were to have their suspicions amply confirmed!

The following evening Dayan called a meeting of the General Staff at his office in Tel Aviv, at which he gave orders to begin mobilising for war against Egypt. He explained that, as a result of the Anglo-French decision to attack the Suez Canal Zone, Israel now had a good opportunity to capture Sinai and break the Egyptian blockade of Eilat. But because of the tension which built up on the Jordan border, Israeli troop movements were interpreted by foreign intelligence services as preliminaries to an attack on Jordan.

The strength of the Israeli Army and Air Force was almost doubled during the final days preceding the Sinai campaign. But while the Israelis were ready to act, the British and French went on squabbling amongst themselves over Operation Musketeer. The British wanted to have nothing to do with any possible link-up with the Israelis. It was the French who wanted it on the assumption that an Israeli operation would bring about the downfall of Nasser. Dayan himself was none too enthusiastic about it. He stood fast in his belief that the Israeli forces could manage very well by themselves. He dismissed Ben-Gurion's concern regarding Egyptian air raids on Tel Aviv and was quite prepared to forego the aid of the British Canberra bombers which were to ground the Egyptian Air Force. He was confident in the ability of the Israeli Air Force to knock out the Egyptian planes before they could penetrate Israel's skies. At the most, he believed, only a few isolated planes would succeed in getting through to bomb Israeli towns. Ben-Gurion was less sanguine on this score and demanded pledges of French or British air protection.

Towards the end of October, Ben-Gurion, Dayan and Peres arrived unobtrusively in Paris and were quickly taken to a private villa at Sèvres to join Mollet, Pineau, Bourgès-Manoury and certain French military leaders.

On the second day of the talks, they were joined by Selwyn Lloyd, the British Foreign Secretary. The French and British were both convinced that the Americans would reconcile themselves to the Suez operation. What worried them was what Russia might do. Ben-Gurion, who was the elder statesman at the meeting, explained to his hosts that they could not rely upon the sympathy, or even inaction, of the Americans. He was quite sure that the United States would not condone the military operation in Suez and would do whatever it could do to express its objection short of using actual force. He also did not believe that any considerations regarding the American Presidential Elections, due to be held on November 5, would deter President Eisenhower. On the other hand, Ben-Gurion was not anxious about the Russians, who were preoccupied at the time with attempting to suppress the revolution which had broken out in Hungary and which they had cause to fear might spread to Poland and East Germany. He did think the Soviet Government would threaten to intervene and even to use missiles, but he predicted it would stop short of resorting to force for fear of a world conflagration which would oblige the United States to take the side of its Western allies.

Ben-Gurion told the British and French that, if they were basing their plans upon a passive American reaction, they would be best advised to call the operation off, for they were likely to be caught with their pants down. Dayan expressed his concern in even stronger terms. He was of the opinion the British were not ready for the operation. After three days of discussions at Sèvres, the Israelis returned home. Two days later, on the evening

159

of October 29, the Sinai campaign was launched.

On that day Shmuel Dayan, Moshe's father, who was a Mapai Member of Parliament, was seen at the Knesset building in Jerusalem, going in and out of the telephone booths, emerging each time with a more anxious look on his lined face. The old man, whose wife, Moshe's mother, had died only a few months before, was overheard mumbling to himself: 'The lad's not there! Where can the lad have got to?' A journalist went up to him and asked him what was wrong. Shmuel Dayan was looking everywhere for his son. The day before Moshe had complained of a cold, and Shmuel was concerned about his health. He did not know that Moshe at that moment was busy running a war, and that the first wave of Israeli paratroops had already captured their objectives in the Sinai desert.

This first paratroop drop took place at the eastern entrance to Mitla Pass, in the mountains between eastern Sinai and the Suez Canal. So preoccupied at that time were Middle East watchers with the tense situation on the Israel-Jordan border that the Egyptian High Command at first judged the Mitla attack to be a mere reprisal raid. Only when armoured columns and infantry thrust into Sinai did the Egyptians and the rest of the world wake up to what was really going on. The timing of the Israeli attack was based on the assumption that the Anglo-French Operation Musketeer, aimed at seizing the Canal Zone, would begin two days later, that is on October 31. The co-ordination of the Sinai invasion with the Anglo-French plan appeared in Dayan's tactics of creating an Israeli threat to the Canal. In his own original plan the emphasis had been on capturing Sharm-el-Sheikh and

London, 1966, Dayan with the Israeli Ambassador,
Aharon Remez (left) and Anthony Greenwood, Minister for
Overseas Development

Vietnam 1966, Dayan as war correspondent fords a river with a U.S. unit

l. to r. Ruth, Assaf, Moshe, Ehud and Yael Dayan. Jerusalem 1950

With the Prime Minister, Levi Eshkol and Deputy Chief of Staff Brigadier Chaim Bar-Lev during a tour of Sinai and Gaza, August 1967

opening the Straits of Tiran. He did not disclose the full truth about the combined Anglo-French-Israeli operation even to his colleagues on the General Staff but contented himself with dropping a few hints. One of these was to compare the Israeli action with a cyclist who gets up a hill by hanging on to the back of a speeding lorry. When they arrive at the crossroads at the top, however, the cyclist lets go and turns off in the direction he wants. Some of Dayan's officers feared the cyclist might slip under the lorry's wheels and be crushed to death. He did not go into such a possibility but declared that, in order to withdraw from somewhere, it was necessary first to be there.

Dayan had set a time-limit of seven to ten days for the completion of the Sinai campaign. This was based on his assessment of his forces' capability of dealing with the Egyptians and, if necessary, any other Arab army which might join in the battle against Israel. In the event, the Egyptians were defeated in Sinai within a week, and no other Arab countries became involved. On the Anglo-French side, however, things did not go quite as had been hoped.

On October 30, Britain and France issued an ultimatum to both Israel and Egypt to stop fighting and withdraw to a distance of ten miles from the Canal on either side. Israel, naturally, agreed to the ultimatum. Nasser rejected it. In the United Nations Security Council, an American resolution calling for a cease-fire and the withdrawal of Israeli troops from Sinai was vetoed by Britain and France. The next day British and French planes began attacking Egyptian air bases. A further cease-fire resolution, adopted by an emergency meeting of the General Assembly, was defied by the two Powers, but it was only on November 5 that Operation Musketeer began in earnest with the dropping of the first British and French paratroops at Port Said. By now, all fighting between Egyptians and Israelis had stopped. On November 6, Anglo-French sea-borne forces took Port Said, but the action had been delayed too long, the game was already up. Under enormous political and economic pressure, particularly from the United States, where Eisenhower had just been re-elected President, Eden threw in the towel. It was the end of his career. The French were clearly disgusted at this dismal failure, which contrasted so strikingly with the brilliant victory achieved by Dayan.

To return to the Israeli side, on the second day of the campaign, Dayan left Brigadier-General Meir Amit, Deputy Chief of Staff, in charge at Headquarters and took over personal command of the operations in the field. Arriving at one of the first objectives which had been taken, Kuseima, midway along the Sinai border, Dayan was furious to discover that the officer commanding the area had sent an armoured brigade into action earlier than the plan called for. Fearing a too-early involvement of his armour with the Egyptians, Dayan raced after the brigade. He found it fanned out across the sand dunes some twenty-five miles inside Sinai, when it should have been some twenty-five miles inside Israel. The tanks, at that moment, looked to him just like a herd of cattle, running away with their tails in the air. It was a momentary flashback to his youth when he used to take his father's herd out to pasture. From the point of view of military discipline, he should have

ordered the brigade to withdraw, but combat circumstances dictated otherwise and he allowed the tanks to
make contact with the enemy. While watching the battle
rage, his eye alighted upon a curious object which had
been unearthed by the tracks of a passing tank. Oblivious
to the heavy shelling going on, he bent down and picked
it up. It was a spearhead made of flint. He was delighted
at his find and remarked with a very knowing wink: 'I
wonder which wild tribe stormed this place thousands of
years ago and sent the inhabitants fleeing in panic,
leaving all their possessions behind.'

Dayan did not miss being in a single critical area
throughout that campaign. He arrived at El Arish in the
midst of fierce fighting and followed the armoured
column as it stormed into the town. Later Dayan stood
with his aides at a window inside one of the buildings
facing the main square, watching the Egyptians surrender
their arms and enter prisoner-of-war stockades. A burst
of machine-gun fire shattered the window, aimed by an
Egyptian sniper hiding in a house opposite. One of
Dayan's aides was killed instantly.

From El Arish, Dayan returned by Piper Cub plane
to headquarters, but as he left the captured town he told
the pilot to fly low to enable him to follow the progress
of the armoured columns making for the Suez Canal. The
plane flew so low that shots were fired at it from rifles and
machine-guns in the hands of Egyptian troops still at
large on the outskirts of the town.

The next day Dayan again turned up at the front.
Near Rafah, Egyptian units were still active, and Dayan
sat with his companions to eat breakfast behind a sand
dune. On that occasion an Egyptian shell smacked into

the dune, splattering Dayan and his aides with sand. Following the advancing Israeli troops, crashing their way through the Egyptian lines, Dayan reached Ali Muntar, a fortified height overlooking the eastern approaches to the town of Gaza. He carefully examined the strength and layout of the fortifications which had just been captured (and which were to spill more Jewish blood in June 1967). Between cracks in the earthworks caused by exploding shells, he found pieces of a human skeleton. For a moment he completely forgot about the battle still raging and dug into the ground. He unearthed a Canaanite grave dating back to the thirteenth century B.C. Inside the grave were a plate and bowl made of clay, placed there as a gift to the dead. When he returned home, these finds were added to his extensive private collection of archaeological relics. Dayan's favourite hobby is to clean and piece together these objects.

The battle did not end with the fall of Gaza and the capture of northern Sinai. The main objective, the occupation of Sharm-el-Sheikh, had still to be accomplished. Dayan had to fight against time, for the hour was rapidly approaching when a vote would be taken at the United Nations requesting an immediate cease-fire. Dayan had to complete the capture of the Tiran Straits before the UN request, which was tantamount to an order, came into effect.

The 9th Infantry Brigade, a unit composed entirely of mobilised reservists under the command of Brigadier-General Avraham Yaffe, left Eilat for the 250-mile journey through the mountainous desert to Sharm-el-Sheikh. On the way they fought minor skirmishes against Egyptian forces stationed along the precipitous route, but their main opponent was the terrain itself, which at times was nearly impassable. Dayan was worried and impatient at the slow rate of progress, and flew to Tor, a small oil-town on the west coast of the Sinai Peninsula opposite the Suez Canal. Israeli paratroops who had landed at Tor were to move off from the town in a south-easterly direction towards Sharm-el-Sheikh, a distance of some sixty miles, in order to link up with the 9th Brigade.

Dayan's plane landed at Tor in the early morning only to find that the paratroops had already moved out on their way to Sharm-el-Sheikh. Never one to be left without something to do, he commandeered several civilian vehicles abandoned by the Egyptians at Tor, collected a few soldiers as an escort and set off in hot pursuit of the advancing paratroops. The area through which he travelled was teeming with thousands of Egyptian troops withdrawing northwards towards Suez. Dayan's small convoy passed the frightened Egyptian soldiers, all fully armed, and not one of them attempted to level his gun at the vehicles speeding by. Dayan, who was sitting next to the driver in a small truck, decided to climb on to the open rear of the vehicle in order to have a better view of the surroundings. In full view of the enemy, and at the mercy of the scorching, mid-day desert sun, Dayan stood up in the truck but ordered his men not to open fire on the Egyptian stragglers so as not to provoke them into a skirmish.

That afternoon, November 5, Dayan followed the paratroops into Sharm-el-Sheikh. The place was already in the hands of the combined forces who had advanced upon it from the north-east and north-west. The Israeli flag was flying from the Egyptian gun emplacement which had prevented Israeli shipping passing through the Straits of Tiran.

That same evening, seven days after the campaign had started, Dayan arrived at Ben-Gurion's home to report the capture and occupation of Sharm-el-Sheikh and the completion of the Sinai campaign. The 'Old Man', who showed visible signs of the strain of the past week, and was also suffering from a heavy cold, looked at Dayan and said with a smile: 'And I suppose you can't stand it, eh?'

Ben-Gurion respected Dayan for his courage. He also knew he could rely upon Dayan to withdraw his forces from the occupied areas when told to do so. The political battle at the United Nations, American pressure, Soviet threats of military action and the failure of Operation Musketeer all made it obvious that Israel would not be able to hold on to the territory she had occupied.

When the Israeli Government decided to withdraw from Sinai, Dayan handed in his resignation as Chief of Staff. But Ben-Gurion refused it, pointing out that it would be understood by public opinion as military pressure against a political decision. Dayan withdrew his resignation and presented it again only nine months later.

However, the seven-day campaign of 1956, and the subsequent deployment of a United Nations force along the Egyptian frontier, rid Israel of the Fedayeen raids and opened the route through Eilat to Africa and Asia. Israel was thus enabled to develop trade and other relations with a number of emerging nations. This at least was a partial substitute for the lack of such relations with her next-door neighbours.

Moshe Dayan emerged from the Sinai campaign a hero

whose praises were loudly and widely sung. Military leaders acclaimed his extraordinary planning and efficient execution. The commander of the U.S. Marine Corps said of him: 'He is an amazing tactician and I'd hate to see him on the enemy's side.' British and other military experts and commanders described him as a master of mobile desert warfare whose thinking and planning were a combination of those of the Second World War heroes, Lord Montgomery and Erwin Rommel. The Sinai campaign served as material for study in senior staff colleges all over the world.

Two days after the victory had been won, and while returning home from a late-night meeting with Ben-Gurion in Jerusalem, Dayan survived an attempt on his life. At one o'clock in the morning he was driving down the winding mountain road from Jerusalem. Ahead of him, in another car, was his aide-de-camp, while behind was a police escort in a third vehicle. As the convoy reached a bend in the road two hand grenades were thrown and a Fedayeen squad opened up with machine-guns. The first two cars managed to get out of range, but the third car was splayed with bullets and its tyres punctured and flattened. However, it managed to continue on its way and limp into Ramleh on its wheel-hubs.

Even before the opening of diplomatic negotiations for the withdrawal of Israel's forces from the occupied areas, Dayan wanted to get the country back to normal. He ordered the demobilisation of all reservist units. Asking his aides to speed up the release of the reserve forces, he said: 'This will not be the last war, and we shall again have to call up our reserve troops. It is better to show the people we do not impose too much upon them.'

The one dark cloud which marred the success of Dayan's campaign was the failure of Operation Musketeer, despite the military success of which it was virtually assured. However, he derived some satisfaction from the knowledge that from the very outset he had been sceptical regarding any tie-up with the British and French. The chances which Dayan had taken in the Sinai campaign were legion, and he made no attempt to hide them from those who criticised his tactical mistakes. In his diary, published nine years later, Dayan writes frankly of these errors, neither does he spare those commanders who erred by acting without orders or contrary to them. He was severely criticised in Israel for these courageous and frank statements and was even accused by some of attempting to denigrate the Israeli Army. Dayan, who more than any other man can justly claim to have created and fostered the Army's fighting spirit, felt he had the right to criticise the performance of his officers, and even of those closest to him. 'Never may one deny the truth, nor delude oneself regarding achievements which never were,' was Dayan's reply to his own critics. The Egyptians are in the habit of bragging and praising themselves for imaginary victories. Dayan certainly did not wish the Israeli Army to emulate them in that respect.

During the months which followed the military victory, Dayan was thrust into a political battle with General Burns, head of the United Nations Emergency Force, who posted observers in Sinai after the withdrawal of Israeli forces. Later he negotiated with Burns over the Israeli withdrawal from the Gaza Strip and Sharm-el-Sheikh. Even when the Israeli forces withdrew from

Sinai, Dayan was with them. He did not wish to desert his men at a time when they would be profoundly distressed as the Israeli flag was lowered. The soldiers who fought under his command did not forget his presence at the frustrating moment of retreat. Israel had finally withdrawn all her troops from the areas occupied in the fighting by March 7, 1957.

Israel's statesmen believed that the UN Emergency Force would act as an effective buffer between Israel and Egypt and would prevent a recurrence of the acts of murder and sabotage inside Israeli territory. Dayan did not share their optimism. As early as August, 1957, he warned against complacency in this respect. The United Nations Emergency Force, he said, would fulfil its function along the borders only as long as Egypt wished to remain passive. He pointed out that the presence of the force depended on the will of Cairo and warned against having any illusions on the subject. He did not content himself merely with issuing warnings but put the Army through its paces with a thorough training programme and stepped up its arms procurement and preparedness. He placed particular emphasis upon strengthening the Air Force. By virtue of the contacts he made with the French on the eve of the Sinai campaign, Dayan saw the chance of strengthening the country's defence potential and was in favour of the initiative taken by Shimon Peres to extend Franco-Israeli co-operation to scientific and technological research. This was to include nuclear research for peaceful purposes.

The year after the Sinai campaign, Ben-Gurion gave his consent to Peres' initiative in opening a window to

West Germany. Peres had managed to establish good relations with Franz-Josef Strauss, then Minister of Defence in the Bonn Government. Through Strauss, the Israeli Minister of Defence obtained equipment which was difficult to obtain from other sources in those days. Together with Peres, Dayan attended one of the secret meetings with Strauss at which they discussed the possibilities of German aid for Israel.

The Israeli arms industry began sending consignments of the Uzzi sub-machine gun, made in Israel, to Germany. This aroused a considerable outcry among the many Israelis who were unhappy about any contact with Germany. The Parliamentary Opposition protested loudly and volubly against the arms deal, and the storm reached its height when one of the Left-wing Opposition parties leaked to the Press the information that a high-ranking official was to be sent to Bonn for talks on arms purchases from West Germany. The official was in fact Moshe Dayan, but he had already been to Bonn before the news leaked out.

Dayan was decidedly in favour of the Ben-Gurion and Peres approach towards the development of good relations with Germany. France was still the only ally Israel had in Europe. Owing to the war in Algeria, France looked upon Israel as a staunch friend, but there was no certainty that this state of things would last for ever. Ben-Gurion hesitated to build the political and security future of Israel upon American orientation. He preferred to rely upon the European nations and the European Common Market which was then being set up. Despite the tragic past between the Jewish and German peoples, Ben-Gurion advocated rising above emotionalism and establishing connections with West Germany, which he saw as a rising power in Europe.

Israel also sought contacts with the new worlds of Africa and Asia. In August 1957, Dayan paid a visit to Africa accompanied by Shimon Peres. Their mission was mainly to ascertain facts and figures concerning requests received from several emerging countries for Israel's technical and military aid. Among the countries they visited were Ghana and Liberia. Later Israel was to supply military advisers to Ghana, Kenya, Tanganyika, the Ivory Coast, Upper Volta, Chad, and the Congo (Leopoldville).

From Africa Dayan and Peres set off for the Far East and visited Burma which was then a firm friend of Israel. On the way back from their official mission, the two men stayed briefly in one of India's main cities. Upon arrival at the sumptuous hotel where they intended staying, the Israelis discovered that the rooms reserved for them had been disposed of. The receptionist was full of apologies but explained that Harold Macmillan, Eden's successor as British Prime Minister, had arrived without notice and had brought a large entourage with him. They had taken an entire floor.

Dayan winked cheekily at the clerk and told him to go upstairs to Macmillan and ask him to give up two of his rooms for the man who had made him Prime Minister. The poor clerk was convinced the one-eyed gentleman was pulling his leg, but Dayan assured him he would not be refused the rooms. The clerk took a look at Dayan's passport and the name somehow struck a chord. He ran upstairs and returned with a member of Macmillan's entourage. The British had understood the hint and offered Dayan and Peres two rooms on the Prime Minister's floor.

When Dayan returned to Israel at the end of the year, he asked to be relieved of his post. Ben-Gurion wanted him to remain a little longer, and Dayan agreed to continue serving in the Army but not as Chief of Staff. In January 1958 he relinquished his post to Major-General Chaim Laskov and took leave to study at the Tel Aviv School of Law and Economics.

From Tel Aviv he went to Jerusalem to attend the Hebrew University, where his daughter, Yael, was also studying. She was by then herself an officer in the Reserve and an up-and-coming writer. While still in uniform, Dayan began expressing his opinions on national affairs. This aroused protests from professional politicians of all parties, including his own. Ben-Gurion ordered him to stop his public appearances, and Dayan decided the time had come to doff his uniform. On November 1, 1958, he resigned from the Army.

In a letter accepting his resignation, Ben-Gurion told Dayan that for several months he had been debating with himself whether or not to do so. He went on to appraise Dayan's devotion and achievements in the service of his country. He referred to Dayan's imprisonment in Acre Gaol, to the loss of his eye, which had not affected the clarity of his vision, to his leadership of the commando battalion in 1948 when he had established the Israeli officer's tradition of commanding 'Follow me!' instead of 'Forward!' The 'Old Man' recalled the day he had appointed Dayan commander in Jerusalem. The officers and men of his former unit had come to Ben-Gurion protesting bitterly at his having deprived them of their commanding officer. 'Since 1948,' Ben-Gurion wrote, 'I have had close contact with you and have recognised that you are endowed not only with outstanding military ability but with the instincts of the diplomat and an unusual degree of statesmanship. These talents you demonstrated in your negotiations with King Abdullah's delegates in the Island of Rhodes, where you gained for Israel the transfer of the railway line to Jerusalem and both sides of the Wadi Ara road.'

Ben-Gurion considered that the climax of Dayan's career was the years of service he had given as Chief of Staff from December 1953 to January 1958. 'The two characteristics,' he wrote, 'with which you are endowed, the ability par excellence to command and your versatile mental capacity, were outstanding during those years, which were years of growing and dangerous tension both on the political front and in the military field. You raised to a high peak the fighting ability of the Israeli Defence Forces, and the climax of your endeavours was the Sinai campaign.'

Having left the Army, Dayan studied political science and modern Middle Eastern history. Parallel with his studies he began to make more and more public appearances. There were those who welcomed the prospect of his joining Israel's political leadership. But some were worried at the challenge with which Moshe Dayan would confront them.

# 9

## The Struggle for the Succession

When Dayan left the armed forces after twenty years of service, he intended plunging straight ahead into the next phase of his public life. He was not one to sit in his ivory tower and wait for the nation to call him out. He was fully aware that the longer he stayed out of the public eye, the wider would the gap grow between him and the man in the street. As an Army officer his contact with non-military people had quite naturally been restricted. His studies occupied only part of his time, and Dayan began devoting more and more attention to public affairs until he found a cause which he considered worth taking up the cudgels for. This was reform of the Government's economic policy. Having chosen his target he went straight at it boldly, without giving a thought to the danger of making himself unpopular.

In the aftermath of the Sinai campaign, the country had plunged into an artificial economic boom. Living standards rose incessantly, demands for higher wages to meet higher costs recurred with constant regularity. The well-to-do grew richer and the State's coffers emptier. Politicians, with an eye on the next elections, buried their heads in the sand, choosing to ignore the dire threat to the future. They did not dare put a stop to the merry-go-round. But Dayan had no desire to join the band-wagon. He severely criticised the country's economic leadership, and in particular the heads of the Histadput (labour federation), whenever he spoke in public. His forthright remarks greatly shocked Mapai members, and the party 'Establishment' began to look upon him as a black sheep. While the party leaders and the Histadrut favoured maximum full employment and an inflationary wage policy, Dayan came out in favour of labour lay-offs and dismissals to create improved efficiency. He demanded anti-strike measures. In 1959 he warned of the time when Israel would no longer be the recipient of financial help from abroad such as German Reparations, grants-in-aid and loans. He suggested a six-year programme which by its nature would create unemployment and lower the standard of living, or at least freeze it, but would place the economy upon a firm and independent base. Dayan's radical proposals anticipated the serious economic crisis into which the country in fact fell six years later, in 1965.

In his campaign against the 'Establishment' both of the State and of his party, Dayan called for reform of the electoral system, which is based on a form of proportional representation, in which votes are cast for nation-wide party lists and not individuals. He demanded a change to constituency representation, on the British pattern. In this he was a faithful disciple of Ben-Gurion, who wished to limit the number of parties represented in the Knesset. Their increasingly large numbers served only to weaken the stability of government. However, Dayan realised from the manner in which the spokesmen of every party recoiled from this idea, that the suggestion was not practical. As an interim measure therefore, he proposed closing the Knesset doors to small parties by establishing

175

a minimum percentage of the national vote which would entitle a party to representation in the House. In this, Dayan gained the support of Ben-Gurion and a group of leaders of the younger generation in Mapai. But Dayan's proposals for strengthening the country's economic structure were met with vociferous denunciations. The loudest decrier was Pinhas Lavon, the powerful Secretary of the Histadrut, whose relations with Dayan had been strained ever since 1954 when they together headed the Defence establishment.

Dayan attacked the policy of the labour federation in acceding to political pressures by establishing wage demands incompatible with either the needs or means of the country. All this brought a shower of invective upon his head. Veteran leaders described Dayan's demands as those of a ragamuffin who 'throws stones at a sacred edifice'. Thus it was not long before he found himself bearing the deprecatory label of 'the thrower of stones at the fifth floor', referring to the floor at Histadrut headquarters where the leaders of the labour federation sat and, to no small extent, decided the fate of Israel's economy. Party oldtimers considered the Histadrut and its institutions to be the symbol of Israel's Socialist progress, but ignored the fact that social and economic conditions had undergone considerable change since the labour federation had established its platform forty years before.

In spite of the objections to Dayan expressed by the Mapai leadership, Ben-Gurion decided to prepare the 'black sheep' for the job of succeeding him. Ben-Gurion was almost 75 when the elections to the Fourth Knesset were held in 1959. He wanted people at the top with

Addressing Arab leaders in Gaza in July 1967

With the Armenian Patriarch
Jeriche Derderian in the Old City of Jerusalem, July 1967

*'We have returned to the holiest of our Holy Places, never again to part from it.'*
Dayan with Brigadiers Narkiss and Bar-Lev at the Western Wall, June 1967

Victory parade, June 1967. Dayan with Chief of Staff Major-General Yitzhak
Rabin (left) and Brigadier Mordechai Hod, Commander of the Air Force

whom he could work in harmony, and could find no common language with his ageing colleagues, though most of them were in fact ten years younger than he. Both in 1953, when he had handed over the reins of office to Sharett and Lavon, and in 1963, when he was to give way to Levi Eskhol, he bowed to the wishes of his party, which did not want to crown Dayan as its leader. But Ben-Gurion nevertheless saw in Dayan, a product of the new Israeli-born generation and a military leader of world-wide renown, the man most suited to succeed him.

In the 1959 elections, Ben-Gurion managed to inject some young blood into the leadership when he placed several people under 50 years old at the top of the Mapai party electoral list, with the intention of getting them into the Government. One of the foremost young men in this group was Moshe Dayan, who represented the forceful approach to matters of foreign and defence policy. As a counter-weight, Abba Eban, who was the same age as Dayan, was also raised to the upper echelons. He had recently returned from his diplomatic post as Israel's Ambassador to the United States and the United Nations. Ben-Gurion's veteran colleagues on the party executive viewed with alarm and dissatisfaction, the 'Old Man's' intention of by-passing them in favour of younger men.

From the very beginning of Dayan and Eban's entry into the political arena the vast difference in the two men was apparent. Eban, born in Cape Town and educated at Cambridge University, spoke in well polished phrases and moderate tones. Dayan spoke in the language of young Israel, in words everyone understood and in a forceful, decisive manner. In an article he wrote then

M

entitled *Inge Toft*, after a Danish vessel of that name
had been arrested by the Egyptians in the Suez Canal
because it was carrying cargo for Israel, Dayan gave
forceful expression to his political outlook. He wrote that
there was no possibility of reaching agreement with
Nasser and, therefore, Israel should pursue a policy of
enmity and aggression towards him. He also envisaged
the possibility of occupying the Sinai Peninsula all the
way to the Canal Zone so as to transform the Canal into
a truly international waterway.

The day of the appearance of this article, Eban announced that Dayan's views were not those of the party.
From then on the political battle between the two men
was joined and quickly became a fierce one.

During his election campaign, Dayan revealed himself
to be a star performer, attracting huge crowds to his
meetings. Only two other speakers could compete with
him in the size of their audiences. One was David Ben-
Gurion and the other Menahem Begin. Dayan is not an
orator as is Begin, neither is he endowed with the appearance of an angry prophet like Ben-Gurion. He does not
possess the mordant wit of Aba Eban. But for his
listeners, and particularly the young people among them,
he is a man who inspires confidence. Those near him
when he stood up to speak could discern a degree of stage
fright. The first few minutes would be full of hesitation,
but once he got into his stride his words would be powerful, direct and lucid, revealing him as a far-sighted
visionary. It was the first time the people had ever seen
him out of his general's uniform, and these public
appearances gained him considerable support. On one
occasion when politicians feared to appear in a Haifa

district, after rioting had broken out there, caused by grievances among new immigrants from Arabic-speaking countries, Dayan walked straight into the district and, from an open-air platform, began a frank discussion with the disgruntled inhabitants. On another occasion he appeared before an audience of 3,000 people in a large square in Petach Tikva. Nearby, addressing an audience of 500, was his old rival, Yigal Allon. There were moments when the voices of the two men drowned each other out as they boomed through the loudspeakers. Dayan then turned to his opponent and invited him to join him on the one platform, with each man presenting his own case. Allon declined.

The veteran leaders who opposed Dayan felt that the 'Old Man' had succeeded in presenting him to the public mind as the nation's future leader. They tried with all their power to block his path, but in 1959 Ben-Gurion still had the final say in his party. In his new Coalition Cabinet, Ben-Gurion gave Dayan the Agriculture portfolio, which he had wanted. It was a chance for Dayan to return to his old stamping ground from which, as the owner of a farm at Nahalal, he had never been completely separated. At the same time Eban became Minister of Education.

Dayan did not deviate from the practices he had adopted in the Army when he took over the Ministry of Agriculture. Seldom did he sit at his desk holding endless discussions. He preferred travelling to those places where things were being done by his Ministry. In his civilian jeep he carried a spade so as not to miss an opportunity of digging into any likely looking mound for archaeological relics. He raced at high speed along the country roads and was involved in several road accidents, although in none of them was anyone seriously injured. When, as the result of one accident, he was charged in court, he had his driving licence suspended for three months. The judge pointed out that the accused, more than any ordinary person, must set an example just as he had done while at the wheel of the country's defences. The judge was, however, lenient with him, emphasising that Dayan had been a faultless driver for twenty-four years, and had demonstrated great civic responsibility and courage in refusing to hide behind his Parliamentary immunity.

Over the years, Dayan's driving habits have become something of a byword in Israel. Both as a general and as a Minister, he would often take the wheel of his own car, even though he had an official driver at his disposal. Once, when the American Senator Stuart Symington visited Israel, he spent some time as Dayan's personal guest. The day Symington was to leave the country, Dayan drove him to the airport in his own Saab car, with the Senator seated beside him in front. At the airport Symington was questioned by journalists who wanted to know what he had discussed with Dayan during the journey. The Senator smiled but said nothing. But Dayan himself chipped in to say that Senator Symington had travelled with the most cautious driver in Israel, so cautious that he had not exchanged a single word with his passenger, for fear that his attention would be distracted from the road. A howl of laughter went up from the assembled journalists, who were well acquainted with the stories of Dayan's impetuous driving.

As Minister of Agriculture, Dayan followed his Army

methods in selecting a team of reliable assistants and handing over to them all organisational and managerial tasks. For himself he kept the main duty of a Minister – the charting of policy and verification that it was being properly carried out. He would be in his office early in the morning, after having already read several newspapers. Usually he would wait for his secretary and assistants to come to his room, listen to the matters requiring his decision, express his opinion in short, succinct sentences, some of which he had formulated in his mind overnight, and give any necessary instructions. He detested and still does detest, the methods of those who try to run everything themselves, even down to the most minor details. Dayan himself believed in delegating authority to his assistants, keeping only major matters in his own hands.

Dayan had become Minister of Agriculture in succession to Kadish Luz, the present Speaker of the Knesset, and a product of the era of Shmuel Dayan, Moshe's father. Dayan's predecessor was a kibbutz member and an idealist respected by everyone, but he found it difficult to withstand the pressure exerted by the various sectors of the agricultural community – the private farmers, the collective kibbutzim and the semi-collective moshavim. Dayan began by trying to impose some order upon this complicated pattern of production.

By the end of the fifties Israel's population numbered two and a half million. The hundreds of agricultural settlements established since 1949 gave rich harvests, so much so that a serious problem of overproduction developed. There were large surpluses of milk, eggs, vegetables and fruit – apart from citrus fruits, which were

Israel's leading export. At the same time there were still large tracts of land lying fallow for lack of irrigation.

Dayan appointed as his assistants economists and experts in the various branches of agriculture. He set up production committees for most branches and laid down production norms for the different branches and sectors in order to adjust production to market capacity, with a view to assuring a livelihood for every farmer.

During his tenure of office, the project of transferring water from the Jordan to the Negev wastes via the national water carrier was put into operation. He had had a hand in the defence of this project while Chief of Staff, when the Syrians endeavoured to prevent by force the diversion of the Jordan waters. Thousands of acres of land had been added to the country's agricultural potential, thus creating additional surpluses. Dayan strove to develop industrial crops, mainly intended for export. At the same time, and in order to reduce excess production and assure a living to those dependent upon agriculture, he decided to shut down the small farms located on the outskirts of towns. This was met with angry protests from cattle owners in the Tel Aviv area, who were forced to slaughter their herds instead of putting them out to pasture alongside the highways leading into the city. He also had an open dispute with the owners of dairies who marketed the produce of the suburban dairy farms. But Dayan's decision was that 'agriculture is for the farmers' and he would not budge an inch despite the pressure exerted upon him.

Even in the poultry branch there were huge surpluses, because the farmers insisted on over-developing this profitable industry. The Minister of Agriculture insisted that a limitation be imposed upon it and that chickens be slaughtered, particularly as the export of Israeli eggs was limited in the extreme. Owners of poultry farms came to protest, but Dayan shrugged his shoulders in a helpless gesture and told them: 'I'm sorry but if the people of Israel don't like eggs, they'll just have to eat chickens.'

But in general terms the farmers were pleased with Dayan's policy and with his concern that they make a reasonable living. He took care to introduce new production methods and suggested abandoning the old, traditional Israeli methods. Israeli farmers, for example, liked to grow the meaty variety of tomato known as the 'Merrimand', which was unsaleable in the world's markets. Dayan suggested growing the 'Moneymaker' variety, which was universally popular. But the farmers would not accept his reasoning and refused to give up their 'Merrimand'. This was one of the few occasions when Dayan threw up his hands in despair and surrendered – to the more meaty tomato!

However, tomatoes excepted, Dayan stood fast in all other matters affecting the future of agriculture within the economic structure of the country. He was entirely devoid of the sentimental attachment to farming which is so often found among the older generation. He is still today a farmer by nature, for he rises at the first light of dawn and often visits his own farm in Nahalal which is run by his elder son, Ehud. Whenever he is there he will lend a hand with the work. He makes good use of farming expressions and comparisons in explaining his ideas. He also has a touch of the thriftiness so characteristic of the farmer, who counts his pennies when he goes to market and is aware that he might be cheated. But, despite his farmer's instincts, Dayan was not blinkered by the idealisation of farming which was so characteristic of the early pioneer settlers in Israel, many of whom gave up academic, professional or business careers for the plough and the pruning knife.

The glut of agricultural produce from which Israel was suffering was aggravated by the fact that most of the world's markets were closed to her. Even the export of citrus was endangered by the restrictions imposed by the European Common Market countries. Dayan foresaw what was coming and suggested that emphasis be placed upon industrial development, while agriculture should be frozen for a time at its current level. Veteran pioneers were furious at such a suggestion from one of their own kind, a product of Degania and Nahalal. Lucidly and logically, Dayan defended his opinions before the Government and was listened to with close attention. But the final word lay with those responsible for planning the economy of the State, the Finance Minister, Levi Eshkol, and the Trade and Industry Minister, Pinhas Sapir. Both Ministers, and especially Eshkol, were in the habit of dealing with any problem by means of committees. All complicated matters were handed over to a committee, from which they often emerged even more complicated. Then they would be referred to another committee. Dayan avoided such bodies like the plague. Whenever he was forced to sit on one he would demonstrate his boredom by brazenly reading a newspaper, much like a rebellious schoolboy during a tedious lesson given by an ageing schoolteacher.

Dayan's relations with the party leaders became more complex from day to day. The oldtimers considered him an upstart who got what he wanted by browbeating others and who ridiculed, or even ignored, whatever they said or did. They were not prepared to grant him credit for any of the achievements of his Ministry, even though farmers of all sectors had expressed satisfaction with his efforts. His proposals for industrialisation did not conflict with his concern to provide the farmer with a decent living. In this context he also took into consideration the welfare of Israel's Arab peasants and of the Bedouin who wandered with their herds from place to place. He wished to put an end to their nomadic existence and provide them with proper housing in permanent settlements supplied with running water and electricity.

The masses lent a ready ear to Dayan's ideas and were impressed by his self-assurance, but the politicians were suspicious of this man whose personality made them flinch. When the Lavon Affair was revived at the end of 1960, and the split between Ben-Gurion and his veteran colleagues came out into the open, Dayan became a target of Ben-Gurion's opponents. The Affair settled back once more into a murky silence after the 1961 elections. Ben-Gurion again assumed the leadership of the Government, and Dayan returned to his post as Minister of Agriculture. But the disharmony within the party hierarchy continued, weakening Ben-Gurion's power and leaving a blemish on the image of Mapai. The Lavon affair created a chasm between Ben-Gurion and his colleagues on the party executive, and Dayan began to make his own way without being dependent upon the Prime Minister's patronage.

However, as long as the 'Old Man' remained at the helm, Dayan was assured of a say in matters of defence and foreign policy. Ben-Gurion did not omit to seek his opinion on any and every question of defence importance which came up for discussion, even though they did not always see eye to eye on them. But on crucial issues such as the furtherance of an independent Israeli deterrent force, Dayan was entirely on Ben-Gurion's side.

Dayan also supported Ben-Gurion's policy of a rapprochement with West Germany, which was implemented by Shimon Peres. He did not become emotionally disoriented as did many in Israel, including Government members, when information was discovered concerning the activities of a number of German scientists and technicians in the development of guided missiles in Egypt. Ben-Gurion and Peres opposed the anti-German campaign which then sprang up, based on demands that Bonn should intervene to prevent the scientists working for Nasser. They had no wish to disrupt the discreet Israeli-German relations before the two countries had exchanged diplomatic missions. Dayan had his own reasons for opposing the anti-German campaign. His was a very realistic assessment of Egypt's limited capacity to build missiles, even with outside assistance. He was also of the opinion that intervention from foreign sources against the Egyptian plan would be of no avail. Therefore, rather than making vociferous but pointless protests, he preferred to mould the country's defences into such a high state of preparedness that they could successfully react to any developments in the area.

But the discussions on Germany, in which Ben-Gurion was pitted against the Foreign Minister, Golda Meir, highlighted the struggle for succession which was going on just beneath the surface. Those members of the party leadership who belonged to the 'in-between' age group and were some ten years younger than Ben-Gurion would not agree to the 'Old Man's' intentions of appointing Dayan and Peres to succeed him. They also displayed their exasperation with Ben-Gurion himself. The debate over Germany, charged as it was with emotion, gave the Prime Minister's opponents a sound excuse for declaring war. Even among his supporters there were those who had reservations over his very positive attitude towards what he called 'this other Germany'. Ben-Gurion's opponents in his own party quickly found allies for their campaign among the members of Ahdut Avoda, who still had old scores to settle with him. Plans were prepared in the strictest secrecy by these two groups. The Mapai veterans wanted to gain control of the party from Ben-Gurion and hand over key posts to the young Ahdut Avoda leaders in order to exclude Ben-Gurion's chosen heirs.

At one stage the oldtimers did, indeed, try to get Dayan on their side, in an effort to gain the support of the younger members of the party and of the farmers and the villagers, all of whom were staunch followers of Dayan. But they were obviously not prepared to pay the price Dayan demanded. Certainly one of his conditions would have been the Defence portfolio, but there were already several claimants to that among the former Palmach and Army officers of Ahdut Avoda. Chief among them was Yigal Allon, Dayan's personal opponent for many years.

In June 1963, Ben-Gurion surprised even his closest associates when, at a meeting of the Cabinet, he announced his resignation as Prime Minister and Minister of Defence. Contrary to what had happened before, this time the majority party, Mapai, did not get involved in lengthy inter-party negotiations before being able to form a Coalition Cabinet. As a matter of fact, the new Cabinet had already been formed. Behind the scenes, the Mapai executive, led by the triumvirate of Levi Eshkol, Golda Meir and Pinhas Sapir, had got together a team which was waiting only for Ben-Gurion to resign.

The suggestion that Eshkol replace the Prime Minister was made by Ben-Gurion himself. Two years later, by which time Ben-Gurion had attacked Eshkol as a leader and pointed out the mistakes he had made in defence matters, the 'Old Man' said that his suggestion had been that Eshkol become Prime Minister only, and that Dayan be appointed Minister of Defence. However, at the meeting of the Mapai executive where Ben-Gurion's resignation was accepted and Eshkol's appointment as his successor approved, the 'Old Man' said not a word about Dayan.

Dayan at first refused to serve as Minister of Agriculture in a Cabinet in which Eshkol was both Prime Minister and Minister of Defence. Explaining his resignation, which he tendered in September 1963, Dayan said: 'Under Ben-Gurion's leadership as Defence Minister, I was happy to serve as Minister of Agriculture, for I knew that defence matters were in good hands.' However, he was prevailed upon to withdraw his resignation, and the new Prime Minister promised to set up a small Ministerial Defence Advisory Committee. This to some extent answered Dayan's complaint that he was not being included in discussions and decisions on defence matters. He hoped to achieve that purpose within the framework of the Committee. Apparently he was to be disappointed. He began showing a lack of interest in staying in the Government and started a campaign against Eshkol's leadership.

Only a few months after the Government had been formed, Dayan came out with a public criticism of the Prime Minister. In a forthright speech, he castigated the methods employed by Eshkol and Sapir, in conjunction with the Histadrut, in matters of economic, and particularly wages, policy. It was not long before his criticisms encompassed matters of general policy and defence.

In 1964, Dayan repeated his warnings on the economy, which he had first voiced in 1959, and drew attention to the rapid erosion of the country's reserves. He again demanded that the Government implement its economic pledges and warned against further rises in living standards and against wage demands which were giving rise to galloping inflation. He demanded stringent and energetic means to increase production and reduce costs, thus enabling Israeli goods to compete on world markets. In response to Dayan's demand, the Prime Minister said, with a smile of rejection, that the Israelis could permit themselves the luxury of a little relaxation. They could, as he put it, wear bedroom slippers and need not always be careering madly towards some goal. Dayan's reply was not long in coming. In a public speech he declared that Israelis must run faster, and even barefoot if they had no shoes. In any event, the time had not yet come for them to relax in bedroom slippers.

Dayan, in company with Peres, also revived his demand for greater industrialisation. His way of thinking was well illustrated by an article he wrote in November 1963, for the London *Jewish Chronicle*, in which he declared:

'Degania, Ein Harod or Nahalal no longer symbolise the vital centres or the problems of our national existence. Those are today symbolised rather by Beersheba, Ashdod or Dimona', that is to say by the growing new urban communities. This article provoked something of a furore in Israel. In the following two years Dayan pressed at Mapai conferences for a re-orientation from agriculture to industry. He did not on these occasions go into great detail about his proposals, although he made it clear that he believed it necessary to get away from the traditional Jewish industries, such as textiles, and to go in for modern, expanding branches of production. However, the Dayan-Peres programme was given some precision in a memorandum which Peres, as Deputy Minister of Defence in Eshkol's Government, submitted to the Prime Minister. This memorandum singled out the electronic, chemical and optical industries as those on which Israel should concentrate on developing.

Another issue over which Dayan differed sharply from Eshkol was the latter's decision, backed by the Mapai old guard, to enter an electoral pact, which was finally signed in May 1965, with Ahdut Avoda, which by now was strongly entrenched in the Coalition Government. Yigal Allon had, in fact, become Minister of Labour in 1961. The so called Alignment which resulted between the two parties was in fact something more than a mere electoral manoeuvre, though it remained less than the reunification which many looked forward to.

Dayan's attacks on the Mapai veterans became increasingly sharp. It was at a meeting packed with junior members of the party, who were his supporters in this struggle, that he first publicly expressed no confidence in Eshkol's leadership. 'What identity card do you have, Mr Eshkol?' he pungently demanded to know.

But Eshkol, confident of wide support in the party, carried the fight into Dayan's own corner. The Mapai organisation gradually began clipping Dayan's wings, and party factotums began searching for material which could be used in the Press to ruin his character. They dug up stories of old love affairs and began a whispering campaign about his alleged over-fondness for women. Dayan's patience was exhausted. In November, 1964, even before Eshkol presented Ben-Gurion's supporters with an ultimatum demanding a declaration of loyalty to himself, Dayan resigned from the Government. This time the step was final.

Ben-Gurion's own campaign against Eshkol had begun when the Prime Minister refused to set up a judicial committee to investigate the Lavon Affair once again and to examine the file which Ben-Gurion had prepared and which, according to the 'Old Man', proved beyond doubt Lavon's responsibility for the 1954 'security mishap'. Eshkol had many reasons for turning the request down. One of the most weighty was the part Eshkol himself had played in setting up the committee of seven Ministers early in 1961 to investigate the matter. According to Ben-Gurion that committee had deviated from the terms of its appointment, for it had cleared Lavon of all complicity without having had any authority to do so. Ben-Gurion believed that in 1961 Eshkol had only wanted to whitewash Lavon so as to avoid a serious crisis in the party executive. For the same reason Eshkol had taken steps to have Lavon removed from the Histadrut leadership. But in 1964, when Eshkol rejected the request for a new investigation, Ben-Gurion began to suspect that already in 1961 the Mapai veteran leaders had been plotting to remove him from the party executive.

After Eshkol refused Ben-Gurion's request, the latter appealed to the Minister of Justice and to the Attorney-General, both of whom favoured the holding of a fresh judicial inquiry. Ben-Gurion would not permit the subject to sink into obscurity. He thereby plunged his party into the worst crisis in its entire history. At the party conference in February 1965, the old guard, led by Eshkol, gained a 60 per cent majority in favour of rejecting Ben-Gurion's demand for a further investigation of the Affair, and in favour of establishing an alignment with Ahdut Avoda. The party functionaries believed that Ben-Gurion would bow to the wishes of the majority and leave well alone. But the 'Old Man' surprised everyone, even his closest associates, by persisting in his struggle. He formed a break-away Knesset faction which several Mapai Members of Parliament joined.

Moshe Dayan was one of those who stood by Ben-Gurion in the early stages of the crisis, but he was not prepared to go so far as to help form a new party. Dayan preferred to remain in Mapai, which had every chance of continuing to be the majority party in the Knesset. He was quite aware of the fact that he had a biological advantage over Mapai's ageing leadership. But Ben-Gurion had the power to demand great sacrifices from his adherents. Eventually Dayan, too, joined Rafi, the new party, although he had not been amongst its first members. In this, Dayan acted as he did in everything, whether in the Army or in political tactics. First he took an exploratory step, and only later plunged right in.

Rafi was organised by Shimon Peres, who was elected its Secretary-General, and Yosef Almogi, who had held the portfolio of Housing and Development in both the Ben-Gurion and the Eshkol Governments. These two bore the brunt of the work, but it was Dayan who was greeted as the leader whenever he put in an occasional appearance at party meetings. Whatever he said was always carefully listened to, and everyone would turn round to look when he sat down in one of the back rows. But he was not interested in the routine details of the new party and did not want to take part in its administration. This attitude infuriated those colleagues who had to do the menial tasks, but the rank and file accepted the leadership of Moshe Dayan as a matter of course.

Dayan was placed seventh in the Rafi list for the Sixth Knesset elections held in November, 1965 but, although Ben-Gurion occupied the place of honour at the top, it was generally understood that Dayan would be the party's future candidate for Prime Minister. But Rafi won only ten of the 120 Knesset seats and its chances of playing a major rôle in the establishment of a Government were nil.

Dayan withdrew from the arena, but it was a tactical withdrawal only, intended to improve his public image. He took up a position as manager of the Yona Fishing Company, a Histadrut-owned enterprise which keeps fishing vessels in the Red Sea. He continued travelling around the country looking for archaeological relics, although it was in a small private car and not an Army or Government vehicle that he now raced along the roads. His colleagues in Rafi complained of the little time he devoted to the new party. But Dayan was after more interesting pursuits.

One opportunity arose when he was commissioned by the Tel Aviv evening newspaper *Maariv* to go to Vietnam and write a number of articles on the war. Left-wing political parties, who demonstrated outside his house in protest against his covering the American side of the war in view of his very special standing in and outside Israel, even brought the matter up in the Knesset (Parliament), obliging the Foreign Minister to explain that no citizen of Israel, even a Major-General and a Member of the Knesset, needs to consult the Government about his private affairs. Dayan ignored his detractors and set off on his journalistic mission, which also gave him an excellent opportunity of keeping up-to-date with his military knowledge.

On his way to Vietnam, Dayan prepared himself with characteristic thoroughness. First he went to Paris and met leading statesmen and Army chiefs who were acquainted with the Vietnamese problem from the days when France ruled the area. He discussed the military side of the problem with General de Castries, who had commanded the French force defeated by the Viet Minh at Dien-Bien-Phu. From Paris he travelled to London for talks with British statesmen and soldiers. In particular he sought the opinion of Field-Marshal Montgomery, whom he considers a great military leader. His next stop was Washington. He talked with the American Defence Secretary, Robert McNamara, and with General Maxwell Taylor, who was then Chairman of the Joint Chiefs of Staff.

Armed with considerable information concerning the political and military background to the Vietnam war, Dayan then left for Saigon. After more background talks with American officers, including General Westmoreland, the Commander-in-Chief, he travelled to Da Nang and went straight to the battlefield. Wearing American battle-dress, he accompanied an infantry reconnaissance unit along jungle paths; he saw from close up skirmishes with the Viet Cong and participated in a helicopter landing. He ate and slept with the troops and, like them, washed his clothing in the same muddy river in which he dipped his perspiring body. He met with farmers in the villages and noted what they had to say and what their grievances were; he took an interest in the American rehabilitation and development projects and returned to Saigon to get answers to his many questions. On his way home he made brief stops in Burma and Thailand to hear what the leaders of those countries had to say about the Vietnam situation and then sat down to write a summary of his impressions in a series of articles which appeared in several newspapers.

It was not only the readers of those newspapers who showed an interest in Dayan's colourful and vivid reports on the Vietnam war. His opinions and impressions carried considerable weight with military men and politicians in Washington. Dayan did not conceal from them his view that there was no hope of ending the war with the methods employed by the United States, even though he did not believe the Viet Cong could win either. American statesmen who were concerned with the situation in Vietnam came to Israel for the express purpose of obtaining Dayan's opinion at first hand. Dayan spoke in public about his Vietnam impressions, but he also lectured at closed meetings to Israeli professional soldiers. It is not known what, if any, of the lessons Dayan had learnt in Vietnam he passed on to the Israeli Defence Forces, but Cairo, at least, had no hesitation in announcing that Dayan had gone to Vietnam to prepare his army for war.

In Israel after his return from Vietnam, he found another front to fight on. The Government had decided upon a policy of economic retrenchment immediately after the elections in November 1965. The country, therefore, was plunged into a serious economic crisis, and Dayan had much to say on the subject. As an anti-inflationary measure, the Government halted many development projects in an effort to create a labour pool and relieve industry of the constant pressure of wage demands. For the very first time, in fact, the Government, backed and aided by the trade union organisation, launched an economic campaign which directly challenged the interests of the workers. Such measures could not have been taken but for the fact that the various Left-wing parties were partners in the Government Coalition. Years before, Dayan had demanded a policy of wage restraint and redeployment to cut production costs and increase productivity. Now, although a member of the Opposition, he could not attack the Government for implementing a policy he himself had advocated in the past. However, as the economic spokesman for Rafi in the Knesset, he accused the Government of bringing on the crisis by breaching its own wage control policy just before the last elections, when millions of pounds had been given in wage increases to Government employees. He also attacked the Government for its handling of the economic restraint policy. This, he claimed, was hurting productive enterprises more than the artificially created projects which, instead of ridding themselves of excess labour, were absorbing the unemployed. Dayan warned against relying upon a leadership which would be incapable of keeping its promises to cure the country's economic ills because of its inherent weakness and craving for popularity. Not many months passed before the Government was forced to revive certain development projects to give work to the thousands of people now unemployed.

That forcefulness which Dayan had demanded in dealing with the economic situation he also demanded in counteracting the El Fatah terror raids. These Arab saboteurs were carrying out murders and attacks on settlements and installations. Opinions were divided in Government circles on the counter-measures to be taken. In certain cases the Government employed strong-arm tactics and in others practised restraint. Some members of the Government advocated passive defence measures such as the erection of a border fence, incorporating an electronic warning system, to protect the railway line to Jerusalem. This was the suggestion after a section of the line had been blown up by mines laid under the track.

Dayan denounced such ideas which, he said, would turn the country into a ghetto behind barbed wire. 'Israel's entire strength lies in her readiness to meet the enemy and crush him before he pounces upon her,' Dayan argued in a discussion on the subject.

Not only did Dayan dismiss the idea of the electronic fence, he also objected to suggestions of appealing to outside forces to mediate between Israel and the Arabs. Instead of employing mediators, Dayan demanded direct confrontation whether in peace or war. 'Ploughman shall face ploughman or soldier shall face soldier,' was his creed. The Arabs must have it clearly explained to them that there were only two possibilities – either to recognise the fact of Israel's existence and to find ways and means of living with her, or to use force against her in an attempt to eliminate her completely. Israel must be prepared for either eventuality but must not give the Arabs a third alternative by agreeing to an outside mediator. 'Israel is not an infant in need of a foreign guardian,' Dayan would say. He would remind his listeners of his willingness in 1957 to permit the stationing of an Egyptian force at Sharm-el-Sheikh in place of the UN Emergency Force, on condition that Egypt guarantee the freedom of navigation in the Gulf of Akaba.

As an Opposition leader, Dayan did not content himself merely with criticising the Government but from time to time would make constructive suggestions. Thus, in January, 1967, he went back to the idea of establishing a confederation between Israel and Jordan along the lines of the 1949 draft agreement with King Abdullah. In an interview published in the newspaper *Haaretz* in January 1967, Dayan suggested that such a confederation would benefit Jordan, cut off as she was from the Mediterranean, even more than Israel. He believed that, unless King Hussein chose to co-operate with Israel, his régime would not be able to hold out much longer against the pressure of Arab nationalist extremism. He proposed that, as part of a deal between the two countries, the problem of the Arab refugees from the 1948 War should be solved by their resettlement on the East Bank of the Jordan. Hussein would be given free access to Israel's Mediterranean ports of Haifa and Ashdod, and there would be joint development of natural resources. Such a confederation could, at a later stage, be extended to include the Lebanon.

However, Dayan did not intend his plan to imply support for the idea of a fusion between Israel and her neighbours. Even if the Arabs had wanted this, he would have rejected the possibility, because of his desire to preserve Israel's distinctive traditions and values and her links with world Jewry. His hope was that within ten years Israel would have a Jewish population of four million (nearly double the present figure), and he looked upon the country as representing Western culture and technology in the Middle East.

'If the Arabs learn to accept the idea that it is not possible to destroy Israel, and that the Middle East is a mosaic and not made of a single hide, they, too, will come to the conclusion that it is possible to compromise and exist together,' was Dayan's opinion. Meanwhile, he suggested that Israel should concentrate on building up her economic strength and efficiency.

As far as domestic politics were concerned, Dayan embarrassed his party colleagues during this period with various suggestions regarding Rafi's future. On one occasion he advocated an alliance with Right-wing parties to form an alternative Government to the Mapai-dominated Coalition. On another he said he saw no independent future for Rafi and hinted at the possibility of making peace with Mapai. His friends interpreted these declarations as political exercises designed to demonstrate that he had not completely withdrawn from the struggle for leadership of the nation.

# 10

## Back in Command

IN THE SPRING of 1967 the storm clouds gathered once again over Israel. In April a long series of Syrian attacks culminated in an air battle in which Israeli jets shot down six Syrian MiG fighters. The following month Egypt began concentrating troops and armour in Sinai. Nevertheless, there was little anxiety in Israel on May 15, the 19th anniversary of the State's foundation. The annual Independence Day military parade was held in Jerusalem. Under the terms of the 1949 armistice agreement with Jordan, restricting military movements in the divided city, the parade was only a small one.

The next day, May 16, all Israel's former Chiefs of Staff were the guests of the current Commander, Major-General Yitzhak Rabin. Present besides Dayan were Yaakov Dori, the first Chief of Staff, now head of the Haifa Technion (Institute of Technology), Professor Yigal Yadin and Mordechai Makleff, Chaim Laskov and Zvi Tzur, respectively in charge of the Dead Sea Works, the Ports Authority and the Mekorot Water Company. Rabin had invited his six predecessors to accompany him on a visit to an Army camp so that they could see for themselves the progress made in combat methods and in the types of equipment at the Army's disposal. In a frank discussion between the seven generals on that spring morning, they analysed the tension along Israel's borders and tried to predict where trouble could next be expected. Most of them held the Egyptian build-up in Sinai to be a mere show of strength, designed to bolster Nasser's prestige against Syrian and Jordanian accusations that he was sheltering behind the United Nations Emergency Force. This indeed was the prevailing Israeli Government view at that moment.

One of the generals voiced concern about the situation on the Syrian frontier. Others feared further guerrilla incursions across the long Jordanian border. But only one concurred when Dayan pointed unerringly at the south as the scene of an impending flare-up. 'Nasser is the real enemy,' said Dayan, 'and it is with him we should mainly concern ourselves. He is launching a new round in his struggle to maintain his position as leader of the Arab world, and this will oblige him to pick up any gauntlet his opponents may throw down. As a first step, he is quite likely to expel the UN force. And his next step may be an attempt to blockade the sea lanes to Eilat.'

Within a matter of days Dayan's forecast proved to be only too accurate, and Israel was faced with the most serious crisis she had known for nineteen years. The United Nations Force had been sent packing from Sinai and the Gaza Strip, Nasser had declared a blockade of Eilat, and seven Egyptian divisions were poised on the frontier. Arab spokesmen, inspired by Nasser's bombast and talk of war against Israel, began to threaten her with annihilation. The Israeli Government suddenly woke up to the gravity of the situation, mobilised the reserves and sent Abba Eban, Golda Meir's successor as Foreign Minister, on an intensive, though unavailing, round of talks in Western capitals. But the Eshkol Cabinet's failure to take firmer measures against the Egyptian menace was interpreted by the public as a sign of weakness and irresolution. Israelis felt that Nasser had carefully studied their leader's shortcomings in timing his action. The suspicion mounted throughout the country that the Egyptian dictator would gain his objectives without having to fire a shot.

Nor did Eshkol's personal demeanour serve to allay these fears, either in the minds of Opposition political leaders, whom he briefed on the situation, or in those of ordinary people. His broadcasts to the nation only deepened the general mood of despair everywhere. Mobilised reservists, returning home for a few hours' leave, expressed impatience with the Government's apparent helplessness. Large advertisements began to appear throughout the politically independent Press calling for the immediate formation of a National Government. Most of these advertisements urged that the War Cabinet should include the '1956 Sinai Campaign Team', meaning Ben-Gurion and Dayan. Among the first public figures to voice such demands were the writers Chaim Hazaz and Natan Alterman. In answer to questions from the newspaper *Haaretz*, a majority of leading scientists and other personalities approached took a similar line. Almost all of them emphasised that Dayan must be given responsibility for defence. Among them was General Laskov. Letters from groups of professional people added weight to this campaign in the Press. At the same time, women whose husbands had already spent a fortnight in the Army demonstrated spontaneously in the streets of the main towns and asked passers-by to sign a petition address-

ed to President Shazar in favour of the establishment of
an Emergency Cabinet. They demanded the return of
Ben-Gurion to the Government, the inclusion of Professor Yigal Yadin, and in particular, the appointment of
Moshe Dayan as Defence Minister.

As public pressure built up in the streets, party leaders
held talks with the Prime Minister with a view to
broadening the Cabinet. The demand to recall Ben-
Gurion as Prime Minister was voiced by none other than
the leader of the Herut Party and former head of the
Irgun Menahem Begin. Throughout his political life,
Begin had been Ben-Gurion's most implacable opponent, but now he swallowed his personal resentment
against Israel's elder statesman. He called upon him
at his home in Tel Aviv and asked him to return to
the leadership of the Government. From there he proceeded to the Prime Minister's Office in Tel Aviv and
asked Eshkol to step down and hand over the reins to his
most virulent critic, David Ben-Gurion.

Begin's demand was refused by Eshkol, but it gained
the support of another Opposition leader, Yosef Saphir,
of the Liberal Party, which is allied with Herut. The
movement to broaden the Cabinet was given an important boost when it was joined by Moshe Chaim Shapira,
Minister of the Interior and leader of the National
Religious Party. While the haggling between the parties
dragged on, Nasser was piling up political gains. King
Hussein, his bitter enemy, flew to Cairo and signed a
military pact which placed the Jordanian Army under
the direct command of an Egyptian general. The stronger
Nasser grew the greater became the public clamour in
Israel for incisive action. Israelis could no longer contain

their disgust at the antics of their politicians at so grave a time. The demand for Dayan's appointment as Defence Minister had by now developed spontaneously into a national movement. And it was joined by a number of leading members of Mapai itself, among them Kadish Luz, Speaker of the Knesset, Abba Hushi, Mayor of Haifa, and Dov Yosef, former Minister of Justice.

But Eshkol and his friends, in particular Golda Meir, who was now Secretary of Mapai, remained utterly opposed to his giving up responsibility for Defence to Dayan. From Eshkol's point of view this would amount to tacit recognition that Dayan had been right in opposing the Prime Minister's action in appointing himself Defence Minister. Eshkol proposed, instead, that Yigal Allon, Minister of Labour, should take over Defence. This, he thought, might satisfy those who wanted a man with military experience. But the Opposition leaders rejected this compromise out of hand. It was Dayan, and Dayan only, they wanted. The National Religious Party and the Independent Liberal Party, both members of the Coalition, agreed with them. When Mapai and Ahdut Avoda Ministers voted in favour of Allon's appointment, Shapira threatened to split the Government. Even Moshe Carmel, Minister of Transport and one of Allon's colleagues in Ahdut Avoda, wanted Dayan. The issue was finally decided at a meeting of the Mapai Secretariat on the morning of June 1. Out of 25 members present, 19 voted for Dayan.

After the decision was taken, several of Dayan's supporters called on him to give him the news and offer their congratulations. Dayan responded with a sardonic laugh, saying his thanks were owed to nobody but the

Egyptian Army. Dayan had not been inactive. For the last fortnight he had, with the permission of the Prime Minister and the Chief of Staff, been touring the country, inspecting military preparations in the Negev, the Jerusalem Hills and Galilee. He had examined plans of campaign and had talks with Army commanders. His visits to front-line troops had done much to raise morale. Several days before his appointment as Defence Minister he had informed Eshkol of his desire to be taken into the Army, stating that he was willing to perform any task and would gladly serve under General Rabin, who in the past had been under his command. He had suggested that he be given command of the southern front. He counselled Eshkol not to hesitate but to hit back immediately at Egypt.

On the evening of June 1, Dayan took part in a short meeting at Ben-Gurion's home in Tel Aviv. Present were leading members of Rafi, some of whom had been high ranking officers in earlier days. Ben-Gurion was not easy in his mind at Dayan's appointment if Eshkol was to remain at the head of the Government. When Dayan got up to leave for his first Cabinet meeting, to which he had been invited by a telephone call from the Prime Minister, Ben-Gurion went up to him, in the manner of a Rabbi to one of his disciples, looked penetratingly at him, shook him warmly by the hand, and said: 'Moshe, put your foot down, and stand for no nonsense.'

The Cabinet meeting ended at one o'clock in the morning. A few hours later Dayan entered the offices of the Ministry of Defence where he found several civilian officials who had been Eshkol's assistants. Dayan could see no point in retaining their services in wartime conditions. Peremptorily, Dr Zvi Dinstein, the Deputy Minister, and some of his civilian helpers were dismissed. One young man, who had been public relations officer at the Ministry, may still not have recovered from the treatment he received at Dayan's hands. When he introduced himself to the new Minister, Dayan, in his inimitable way, scrutinised his smooth, almost beardless features and said with a smile, 'Go home, lad, there's a war on here now.' In place of the civilians, Dayan appointed as his Special Assistant General Zvi Tzur.

The same day, June 2, that he took command of the Ministry offices, Dayan walked into Army Headquarters. Standing around a map-table were several officers who, since he had left the Army, had risen several ranks. They greeted him with friendly smiles, although it was clear to them that they would have no easy time with him. But it was equally obvious to them that, at such a time, they needed a man who would listen to what they had to say and then give them a definite decision. Dayan saw the question in their faces. Unceremoniously he told them: 'Gentlemen, I know exactly what your opinion is of me, and you certainly know what my opinion is of you. I suggest that now you think along the lines I am thinking . . .' Three days later Israel replied to the Egyptian challenge. The Six-Day War had begun.

Up till the evening of June 1, the Cabinet had been divided over what measures to take Eshkol himself hesitated to opt for military action, even though the military commanders urged upon him its chances of success. On May 27, Abba Eban, the Foreign Minister, had returned from his visits to London, Paris and Washington, where he had been seeking a political solution to the crisis. Eban urged the Cabinet to accede to President Johnson's request to delay any action pending the proposed formation of an international convoy to test the blockade of Eilat. At the Cabinet meeting held on the day of Eban's return Eshkol refrained from asking his colleagues for a final decision. Instead, he held a trial vote. In this vote, as Eshkol later disclosed, the Cabinet was equally divided, nine Ministers in favour of waiting, in accordance with the American President's request, and nine in favour of immediate action. The Prime Minister himself is believed to have been among the latter. But he postponed the final decision until the next day. In the meantime he received a further message from Johnson pleading for patience, although it was already clear that the international convoy project was running into difficulties, and it was doubtful whether the President would succeed in carrying out his promises in that direction. Nevertheless, the message had an effect on Eshkol, and at the Cabinet meeting on May 28 he counselled waiting. This time there was no vote. The only Minister who opposed the Prime Minister's advice and demanded instant action was Moshe Carmel.

That was on a Sunday night. The Government's hesitation continued for most of the week. On Thursday night, June 1, the Cabinet met again. Present were its newly co-opted members, Moshe Dayan and Menahem Begin (Yosef Saphir, too, was to join it slightly later). At that meeting, as a veteran Minister told the author of this book, a new atmosphere could already be felt. A further meeting took place the next day, and this time, instead of abstract discussions on whether 'to act or not to act', Dayan put forward concrete proposals about what should be done. From that moment it was clear that the question of whether any action should be taken had been resolved. Only the question of timing remained open.

At his first Press conference as Minister of Defence, Dayan succeeded in misleading the world, which was awaiting immediate Israeli action, by saying: 'It is too early or too late.' This statement persuaded many of the hundreds of foreign correspondents in the country to return home on the eve of war. On the same occasion Dayan affirmed Israel's readiness to defend herself without foreign assistance. 'We do not want Americans or others to be killed for our cause,' he said.

The Army was ready for any Egyptian attack, but the operational plans which had been prepared were on a limited scale and, surprisingly, provided only for the occupation of Gaza and northern Sinai, with the aim of crushing the bulk of the Egyptian Army. They left out of account Sharm-el-Sheikh. Dayan thought it absurd to fight without taking Sharm-el-Sheikh and thus breaking the blockade of Eilat which, in the eyes of the world, was the initial act of aggression which justified Israeli retaliation. As soon as he became Defence Minister, Dayan gave orders to set up a task force to achieve this aim. When everything was ready, in accordance with the amended plans, now providing for the capture of the whole of Sinai, the Cabinet met on Sunday, June 4, and took the fateful decision which, by the end of that week, had changed the map of the Middle East.

When, on Monday morning, fighting broke out on the Egyptian front, no plans had been made to deal with a general onslaught by King Hussein's forces, which was not expected. There were preparations to repulse localised attacks but not to occupy Jordanian territory. However, after mounting Jordanian attacks on that first day, Dayan gave direct instructions to the commander of the central front, Brigadier-General Uzzi Narkiss, to throw into action a detachment of tanks stationed in the hills about nine miles west of Jerusalem. Full-scale war thereupon broke out on the West Bank of the Jordan. An Israeli division, withdrawn from the northern front, pierced Jordanian defences in the Jenin sector and advanced to Nablus, where it met the Israeli tank forces coming from the south. Jordanian and Iraqi forces finally retreated across the river on Thursday, June 8.

The Israeli public was not informed about the successes of their forces until the early hours of the morning of June 6, as Dayan's policy had been to hold back news of the fighting during the first and decisive day of the War. This was in order, not only to mislead the Egyptian Intelligence, but to prevent the friends of the Arabs in the United Nations from trying to enforce an immediate ceasefire, which would have saved the Egyptian Army from collapse. One result of this was that on the evening of June 5 the Soviet Ambassador to Israel, Dmitri Chubachin, sought an urgent meeting with the Foreign Minister, Abba Eban, at which he warned him of the terrible blow the Egyptians were about to deliver against Israel.

When, on June 7, Dayan finally faced the press for the first time since the beginning of the War, he was able to confirm that most objectives had been taken within the first sixty hours.

Thus Dayan had not only played a vital role in deciding the operation against Egypt and extending its scope, he was also directly responsible for the steps which led to the conquest of the whole of the West Bank of the Jordan. In contrast to the speed with which he acted on the central front, Dayan delayed action against Syria, while the division from Northern Command was busy on the West Bank. Only on the morning of Friday, June 9, did Israeli forces storm the Golan Heights, from which for so long the Syrian Army had harassed the settlements of northern Galilee. Here again Dayan went beyond the original plans, which had envisaged penetrating only five miles into Syrian territory. Acting on his instructions, Israeli forces drove the Syrians beyond the line from Kuneitra to Butmiye, making sure that all Israel's territory would be safe from Syrian long-range artillery.

The emotional climax of the Six-Day War was undoubtedly the capture by Israeli paratroops of the Wailing Wall in the Old City of Jerusalem. While the troops were standing there, their guns leaning against the wall, their heads pressed against the age-old stones, Dayan appeared on the scene together with the Chief of Staff and commanders of the central front, all wearing steel helmets. While bullets still whined along the narrow streets of the Old City, Dayan became the first national leader to declare from the Wailing Wall: 'We have returned to the holiest of our holy places, never again to part from it'.

Dayan's declaration virtually established Government policy in the coming days. Even before other leaders had had time to formulate or express their opinions on the happenings which had brought about so sudden a transformation in the prestige and problems of Israel,

Dayan had set the policy and made the rest of the Government follow his lead.

A week after the victory, Moshe Dayan was lying in a deckchair in the garden of his home at Zahala, a Tel Aviv suburb. Next to him stood a bowl of ripe red plums he had plucked from his trees for his guests. Round about was spread his collection of antique statuary. It was late in the evening and only the buzzing of insects whirling around the electric lamp disturbed the silence. Dayan was thinking, gazing up into the star-spangled night. Suddenly he asked as though trying to convince himself: 'Could it have been possible a week ago to imagine such boundaries as these or such security as this?'

He got up from his chair, sat down again, constantly changed position, crossed and uncrossed his legs, fidgeted with the ribbon of his black eye-patch, repeating the same gestures again and again. It was obvious that his thoughts were disturbing him. Preying on his mind was the Arab problem. In Dayan's opinion this is the greatest test the State must face, now that military victory has been achieved. Now, as formerly, he favours direct confrontation with the Arabs. After the Six-Day War he stopped thinking in terms of a confederation with Jordan and began to strive towards a direct partnership between Israel and the Arabs in the new areas. A few days after the war he took a trip to the Arab-populated areas in order to try to make contacts directly with Arab intellectuals, religious leaders and other personalities whom he believed to be potential leaders of the West Bank and Gaza Strip communities. Dayan's view is that the Palestinian Arabs themselves must decide their own future, without recourse to Hussein or Nasser, both of whom used them as political pawns and never bothered to satisfy their real needs.

Despite a variety of statements attributed to him since the end of the Six-Day War, not all wholly consistent with each other, Dayan's basic attitude remains that Israel must give maximum freedom to the Arab communities in the occupied areas, subject to the condition that terrorism must be firmly suppressed. He urges that there should be freedom of movement between Israel and the Arab areas and to some extent – completely, in the case of Jerusalem – this has been achieved. His intention was to demonstrate to the Arabs that Israel can assure their civic and economic liberty and wellbeing. At the same time, he opposed the return of those Arabs who chose to flee from the West Bank. He loses no opportunity of emphasising the historical ties which bind the Jewish people to the occupied areas. However, in the absence of any political settlement with Israel's Arab neighbours, his inclination is towards giving the West Bank a limited autonomy. Any outright annexation, he fears, would tilt the demographic balance too much in favour of the Arabs, with their higher birth rate.

The Arabs, who had previously respected Dayan as a military leader, also found in him after the Six-Day War a man who could talk to them in their own language and who could understand their problems, whether as farmers or merchants. He soon gained considerable popularity among them. Six weeks after the war, at a wedding reception held at his home, Arab sheikhs could be seen tasting oriental delicacies and mixing with foreign diplomats, Israeli Cabinet Ministers and senior Army officers.

The wedding was a double one: that of his daughter Yael to Colonel Dov Sion, to whom she had become engaged in a whirlwind courtship while on active service in Sinai the month before; and of his younger son Assaf to Aharona Malkind, who had just finished her Army service. By now Yael, with several books behind her, was commonly spoken of as the Israeli 'Françoise Sagan', while Assaf was a promising young actor.

Dayan's public statements on the Arab problem, particularly on the refugees, aroused heated debate. His opponents accused him of irresponsibility. Indeed, almost as soon as the war was over, Israel's internal political strife started up again with renewed vigour. Dayan's detractors resumed their accusations that he was an adventurer and a danger to democracy, apparently basing themselves upon his impatience with red tape and his undisguised preference for people who are 'doers' rather than talkers They tried to belittle his contribution to victory and even held against him the manner in which he had entered the Government, regarding the wave of popular pressure which brought him to power as some kind of 'putsch'. The higher Dayan's dynamism carried him in popular esteem, the greater became the anxiety among his political rivals in Mapai and Ahdut Avoda.

Negotiations which began after the war for a three-way merger of Mapai, Rafi and Ahdut Avoda dragged on for six months until January, 1968, when they finally came together to form the Israeli Labour Party. Behind all the points of organisation, ideology and economic policy which came into the arguments between the three parties lay the latent struggle for the succession to power between

Yigal Allon and Moshe Dayan. There seems every likelihood, at the moment of writing that Eshkol will retain the leadership of the new party at least until the 1969 General Election. Another possible compromise candidate for the Premiership might be Pinhas Sapir, or even Abba Eban. But, whichever way the wind blows, Dayan will remain a formidable contender.

In the meantime, Dayan's is the voice that has been listened to with most attention, both in Israel and abroad, as far as problems of security are concerned. In a newspaper interview in January, 1968, he forecast that, if diplomatic pressure failed to make Israel withdraw from Sinai without attaining her stated objective of a peace treaty, Egypt would resort to war again. He was confident Israel would again win but he could not promise it would be a 'de luxe' war. In any case, he added, Egypt would not act without the agreement of the Russians who had now all but taken charge of her military machine. Dayan also took the opportunity of stating his views on the future of Arab-Israeli relations when, in the same month of January, he addressed several hundred Egyptian prisoners-of-war just before their repatriation. He told the Egyptians, including nine generals, that they would never succeed in wiping Israel off the map. Instead he offered them the prospect of peaceful co-existence, on the basis of mutual respect. The basic points of any such settlement, Dayan insists, must be secure and agreed borders and Israeli freedom of navigation in the Tiran Straits and the Suez Canal.

In his private life, as in his political career, Dayan has always been something of a lone wolf. Although very attached to his family, Dayan has spent long periods in virtual isolation from them. Particularly during his years at the head of the Army, he was said to use his home merely as a hotel. It was this which gave rise to talk of his estrangement from his wife Ruth. But, after such periods, the couple would always be seen together again, at a theatre or a reception. Ruth Dayan is also often seen with her husband in the company of his political friends, although she herself is not politically active. She is, however, very independent and a personality in her own right. She founded the Maskit company, which specialises in the production of traditional garments worn by Jewish immigrants from such countries as the Yemen and Morocco. She has established handicraft centres in the immigrant villages and looks after the sales of these goods both in Israel and abroad.

With his children, Dayan was a strict disciplinarian, laying down almost military rules for them, and this was felt even during his absences. In his spare moments he would take the children into the fields and teach them how to handle a gun and shoot wild pigeons. He guided their reading towards the Russian classics he had himself enjoyed as a youngster, and bitter would have been the fate of any of them he caught reading a penny-dreadful instead.

Dayan has few friends, and his social life is almost entirely restricted to public and artistic functions, although when he is in company he quickly becomes the centre of interest, with politicians, military men, artists, philosophers and attractive young women crowding round him. But he has not mastered the art of patience. When he loses interest in his companions he makes no attempt to conceal his irritation, pacing up and down and fiddling with his eye-patch. Even at a reception given in his own honour he will sometimes walk out without offering apologies to anyone.

He enjoys listening to good music and seeing *avant-garde* plays and has a penchant for wide-screen war films. He does not frequent cafés, does not smoke and drinks very rarely. When he reads a book it is usually a work of history or archaeology. He is most relaxed when he is by himself, trying to piece together the fragments of some article of Canaanite pottery which he has found to add to the hundreds of relics in his collection.

When he has nothing to do, when he has no interesting challenge to meet, Dayan displays obvious signs of frustration and annoyance. These may make their appearance even when he is at home in Zahala with his family. Then he will go off by himself into his garden or shut himself up in his extensive library. On such occasions, when he is bottled up within himself, even his wife and three children are likely to find themselves strangers to him, and only his baby granddaughter, Gal, is able to bring a smile to his lips. Yael Dayan says of her father: 'He is a lonely man who holds the key to his soul in his own hand, and he himself directs the traffic of people and ideas trying to reach him.'

Dayan is still liable to retire into his corner. He may go into seclusion and write, he may manage a business enterprise, he may go off on archaeological expeditions. It would be out of character for him to resort to party political scheming to ensure his place at the top. Yet, after the Six-Day War and after the renown he has won as a soldier and statesman of vision and determination, it would be difficult to imagine the future leadership of Israel without Moshe Dayan at its centre.

The esteem in which Moshe Dayan is held amongst the Israeli people was shown once again on March 20, 1968, when Dayan was involved in a serious accident, news of which spread like wild-fire throughout the country several hours before any official announcement. The accident occurred on the day when the Government had decided to take action against terrorist attacks carried out by El Fatah gangs based on the eastern bank of the Jordan river. It was planned to blow up several terrorist bases at Karame, avoiding contact with the Jordanian army if at all possible.

As is his habit after taking vital decisions, Dayan was relaxing at his main hobby, archaeology. He was digging for sherds of Canaanite pottery, when there was a sudden landslide and a ton of earth covered him completely. Within seconds of the accident, children, who were always present when Dayan made an appearance at an archaeological site, had alerted the other members of the team and in less than two minutes Dayan's head had been freed. His first words were to ask after the welfare of the young assistant who always accompanies him on these excavations; and who was, in fact, lucky enough to escape unharmed.

Dayan was rushed to hospital where doctors were waiting for him in the emergency room ready to give immediate first-aid. He was semi-conscious, and in great pain, but he was in such control of himself that only the medical staff who have daily experience of such accidents could perceive how much he was suffering.

Before allowing them to attend to him he asked gruffly for a pain reliever . . . and a telephone. Only after he had made several important calls, dialling the numbers from memory, and had given the necessary instructions, would he let the medical staff deal with his injuries. Later when the chief of the hospital, Professor Chaim Shiba, was asked about his patient, he replied: 'He behaves like a hero, just like Moshe Dayan.'

# INDEX

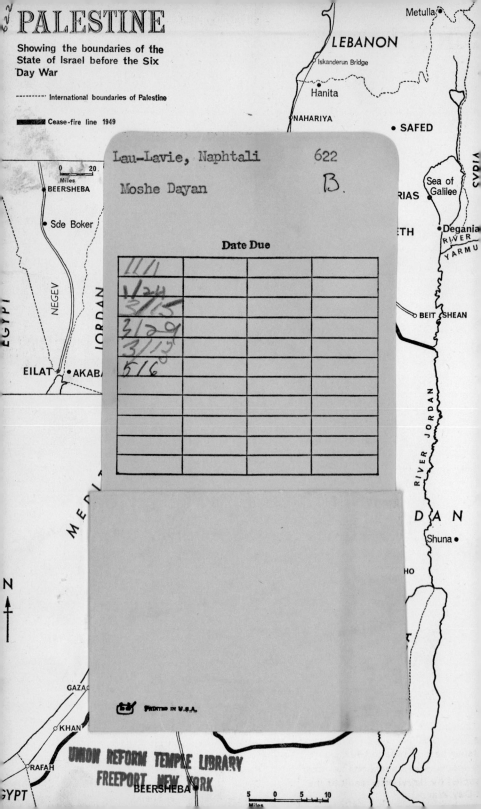